D1528521

Miranda Rights

POINT / COUNTERPOINT

Affirmative Action

Amateur Athletics

American Military Policy

Animal Rights

Capital Punishment

DNA Evidence

Election Reform

The FCC and Regulating Indecency

Fetal Rights

Freedom of Speech

Gay Rights

Gun Control

Immigrants' Rights After 9/11

Immigration Policy

Legalizing Marijuana

Mandatory Military Service

Media Bias

Mental Health Reform

Miranda Rights

Open Government

Physician-Assisted Suicide

Policing the Internet

Protecting Ideas

Religion in Public Schools

Rights of Students

The Right to Privacy

Search and Seizure

Smoking Bans

Stem Cell Research and Cloning

Tort Reform

Trial of Juveniles as Adults

The War on Terror

Welfare Reform

Miranda Rights

Paul Ruschmann, J. D.

SERIES CONSULTING EDITOR
Alan Marzilli, M.A., J.D.

CHELSEA HOUSE
PUBLISHERS
An imprint of Infobase Publishing

Miranda Rights

Chelsea House
An imprint of Infobase Publishing
132 West 31st Street
New York NY 10001

ISBN-13: 978-0-7910-9229-3
ISBN-10: 0-7910-9229-1

Library of Congress Cataloging-in-Publication Data

Ruschmann, Paul.
  Miranda rights / Paul Ruschmann.
      p. cm. — (Point-counterpoint (Philadelphia, Pa.))
  Includes bibliographical references and index.
  ISBN 0-7910-9229-1 (hardcover)
  1. Miranda, Ernesto—Trials, litigation, etc. 2. Trials (Rape)—Arizona. 3. Right to counsel—United States. 4. Self incrimination—United States. 5. Confession (Law)—United States. 6. Police questioning—United States. I. Title. II. Series.

  KF224.M54R87 2006
  345.73'056—dc22   2006017147

Chelsea House books are available at special discounts when purchased in bulk quantities for businesses, associations, institutions, or sales promotions. Please call our Special Sales Department in New York at (212) 967-8800 or (800) 322-8755.

You can find Chelsea House on the World Wide Web at
http://www.chelseahouse.com

Series and cover design by Takeshi Takahashi

Printed in the United States of America

Bang Hermitage 10 9 8 7 6 5 4 3 2 1

This book is printed on acid-free paper.

All links and Web addresses were checked and verified to be correct at the time of publication. Because of the dynamic nature of the Web, some addresses and links may have changed since publication and may no longer be valid.

\\||||||CONTENTS

Foreword

Alan Marzilli, M.A., J.D.
Washington, D.C.

The debates presented in POINT/COUNTERPOINT are among the most interesting and controversial in contemporary American society, but studying them is more than an academic activity. They affect every citizen; they are the issues that today's leaders debate and tomorrow's will decide. The reader may one day play a central role in resolving them.

Why study both sides of the debate? It's possible that the reader will not yet have formed any opinion at all on the subject of this volume—but this is unlikely. It is more likely that the reader will already hold an opinion, probably a strong one, and very probably one formed without full exposure to the arguments of the other side. It is rare to hear an argument presented in a balanced way, and it is easy to form an opinion on too little information; these books will help to fill in the informational gaps that can never be avoided. More important, though, is the practical function of the series: Skillful argumentation requires a thorough knowledge of *both* sides—though there are seldom only two, and only by knowing what an opponent is likely to assert can one form an articulate response.

Perhaps more important is that listening to the other side sometimes helps one to see an opponent's arguments in a more human way. For example, Sister Helen Prejean, one of the nation's most visible opponents of capital punishment, has been deeply affected by her interactions with the families of murder victims. Seeing the families' grief and pain, she understands much better why people support the death penalty, and she is able to carry out her advocacy with a greater sensitivity to the needs and beliefs of those who do not agree with her. Her relativism, in turn, lends credibility to her work. Dismissing the other side of the argument as totally without merit can be too easy—it is far more useful to understand the nature of the controversy and the reasons *why* the issue defies resolution.

The most controversial issues of all are often those that center on a constitutional right. The Bill of Rights—the first ten amendments to the U.S. Constitution—spells out some of the most fundamental rights that distinguish the governmental system of the United States from those that allow fewer (or other) freedoms. But the sparsely worded document is open to interpretation, and clauses of only a few words are often at the heart of national debates. The Bill of Rights was meant to protect individual liberties; but the needs of some individuals clash with those of society as a whole, and when this happens someone has to decide where to draw the line. Thus the Constitution becomes a battleground between the rights of individuals to do as they please and the responsibility of the government to protect its citizens. The First Amendment's guarantee of "freedom of speech," for example, leads to a number of difficult questions. Some forms of expression, such as burning an American flag, lead to public outrage—but nevertheless are said to be protected by the First Amendment. Other types of expression that most people find objectionable, such as sexually explicit material involving children, are not protected because they are considered harmful. The question is not only where to draw the line, but how to do this without infringing on the personal liberties on which the United States was built.

The Bill of Rights raises many other questions about individual rights and the societal "good." Is a prayer before a high school football game an "establishment of religion" prohibited by the First Amendment? Does the Second Amendment's promise of "the right to bear arms" include concealed handguns? Is stopping and frisking someone standing on a corner known to be frequented by drug dealers a form of "unreasonable search and seizure" in violation of the Fourth Amendment? Although the nine-member U.S. Supreme Court has the ultimate authority in interpreting the Constitution, its answers do not always satisfy the public. When a group of nine people—sometimes by a five-to-four vote—makes a decision that affects the lives of hundreds of millions, public outcry can be expected. And the composition of the Court does change over time, so even a landmark decision is not guaranteed to stand forever. The limits of constitutional protection are always in flux.

These issues make headlines, divide courts, and decide elections. They are the questions most worthy of national debate, and this series aims to cover them as thoroughly as possible. Each volume sets out some of the key arguments surrounding a particular issue, even some views that most people consider extreme or radical—but presents a balanced perspective on the issue. Excerpts from the relevant laws and judicial opinions and references to central concepts, source material, and advocacy groups help the reader to explore the issues even further and to read "the letter of the law" just as the legislatures and the courts have established it.

It may seem that some debates—such as those over capital punishment and abortion, debates with a strong moral component—will never be resolved. But American history offers numerous examples of controversies that once seemed insurmountable but now are effectively settled, even if only on the surface. Abolitionists met with widespread resistance to their efforts to end slavery, and the controversy over that issue threatened to cleave the nation in two; but today public debate over the merits of slavery would be unthinkable, though racial inequalities still plague the nation. Similarly unthinkable at one time was suffrage for women and minorities, but this is now a matter of course. Distributing information about contraception once was a crime. Societies change, and attitudes change, and new questions of social justice are raised constantly while the old ones fade into irrelevancy.

Whatever the root of the controversy, the books in POINT/ COUNTERPOINT seek to explain to the reader the origins of the debate, the current state of the law, and the arguments on both sides. The goal of the series is to inform the reader about the issues facing not only American politicians, but all of the nation's citizens, and to encourage the reader to become more actively involved in resolving these debates, as a voter, a concerned citizen, a journalist, an activist, or an elected official. Democracy is based on education, and every voice counts—so every opinion must be an informed one.

On television dramas, police officers recite the familiar words, beginning with "You have the right to remain silent," in such a deadpan way that viewers are led to believe that the Miranda warnings are just a fact of life in police work. However, the U.S. Supreme Court's *Miranda* decision, requiring police officers to read these warnings, caused a furor in 1966, both among police forces and members of the public supporting law and order. Though the warnings have been given countless times over the last four decades, many continue to criticize how the legal system treats police interrogations. Some people argue that short of torture or threats, police should have great leeway in getting suspects to confess. Others argue that the Miranda warnings do not sufficiently protect the rights of the accused. This volume explains the origin of the Miranda warnings and examines the arguments on both sides of the debate over their continued relevance in a society threatened by violent crime and terrorism.

Miranda v. Arizona

*M*iranda v. Arizona, which requires police officers to advise suspected criminals of their rights before questioning them, is one of the most famous decisions ever handed down by the United States Supreme Court. "Miranda warnings" have been recited so many times by characters in televised police dramas and in movies that they are part of American popular culture. The words "you have the right to remain silent" are familiar to millions of people around the world. Even children can recite them from memory.

Miranda is also famous for the debate it provoked. Advocates for the accused called it a much-needed measure to curb police misconduct, but the law-enforcement community argued that it prevented the police from doing their job. Judicial liberals hailed *Miranda* as part of the "due process revolution" that forced the government to deal more fairly with citizens, whereas conservatives accused the Court of having wielded power that rightfully belonged to the people and their elected lawmakers. *Miranda* was also a symbol of the turbulent politics of the late 1960s. Supporters viewed it as another step toward a more equal society, and opponents saw it as yet another sign of a more lawless America.

The State of Arizona v. Ernesto Miranda

The *Miranda* case began on March 3, 1963, when a young woman called "Jane Smith" (accounts of this case use a false name to conceal her identity) told the police in Phoenix, Arizona, that she had been abducted and sexually assaulted. She described her attacker as a small, light-skinned man of Mexican descent. At first, the police had few facts on which they could build a case. Later, however, Smith's brother-in-law noticed an old Packard car

The *Miranda* Rights Card Carried by Phoenix Police

You have the right to remain silent.

Anything you say can be used against you in a court of law.

You have the right to the presence of an attorney to assist you prior to questioning and to be with you during questioning if you so desire.

If you cannot afford an attorney you have the right to have an attorney appointed for you prior to questioning.

Do you understand these rights?

Will you voluntarily answer my questions?

Source: Liva Baker, *Miranda: Crime, Law, and Politics*. New York: Atheneum, 1983, pp. 177–178.

cruising the area near the location where she had been abducted. He took down the license plate number and reported it to the police. They traced the car to Ernesto Miranda's common-law wife, Twila Hoffman. Miranda fit Smith's description, and he already had a police record and had spent time in prison.

The police took Miranda to the police station and put him in a lineup, where Jane Smith tentatively identified him as her attacker. They then brought Miranda into an interrogation room. After two hours of questioning, Miranda confessed. In his book about the *Miranda* case, lawyer Gary Stuart described what happened:

> Noting the gravity of the officer's demeanor, Miranda shifted uneasily in his chair and asked, "How did I do?"
>
> "Not too good, Ernie," replied [Detective Carroll] Cooley, noticing Miranda's concern.
>
> "They identified me then?" Miranda asked.
>
> "Yes, Ernie, they did," Cooley replied gravely.
>
> "Well," said Miranda resignedly, "I guess I'd better tell you about it then."[1]

Miranda told the detectives about the night he assaulted Smith, and some of the details of his confession matched those given by his victim. He also admitted to having attacked two other young women. After confessing, Miranda wrote and signed a one-paragraph statement. At the top of it was a typed paragraph that read as follows: "I, _____, do hereby swear that I make this statement voluntarily and of my own free will, with no threats, coercion, or promises of immunity, and with full knowledge of my legal rights, understanding any statement can be used against me."[2]

After Miranda confessed, he was charged with kidnapping and raping Smith and with robbing another woman, "Susan Jones." (He also confessed to kidnapping and robbing a third victim, "Mary Brown," but he was not charged.) In the rape case, the evidence against Miranda consisted of the statement he made to the police and the testimony of the victim and the detectives. Miranda's lawyer argued to the jury that the police violated his client's constitutional rights in obtaining his confession, but the jury found Miranda guilty anyway. The day before, a different jury had convicted Miranda of robbing Susan Jones. The judge sent him to prison for both crimes. Miranda's lawyer appealed his rape conviction on the grounds that the police acted unlawfully in obtaining his confession. In *State v. Miranda*, the Supreme Court of Arizona turned down his appeal. In doing so, it concluded that Miranda's confession was voluntary. Under normal circumstances, that would have been the end of the case, but the law governing confessions was beginning a transition.

The Legal Road to *Miranda*

In the 30 years before Ernesto Miranda was tried, the legal standard as to when a defendant's confession should be allowed into evidence had changed greatly. That was in large part because two racially charged criminal cases had caused the Supreme Court to reverse its long-standing "hands-off" approach, in which criminal cases decided in state courts were not considered to be under the Court's purview. In 1932, in *Powell v. Alabama*, the Supreme Court overturned the convictions of four young African Americans who had been denied effective legal representation at their trial. Four years later, in *Brown v. Mississippi*, the Court overturned the conviction of three African-American sharecroppers because their confessions had been obtained through torture.

After *Brown*, the Supreme Court took up a series of cases in which the issue was whether the manner in which the police got a defendant to confess violated his or her constitutional rights. The Court gradually expanded the grounds for excluding a confession from evidence. Tactics such as extended nonstop interrogation, injecting truth serum, passing off a government psychiatrist as a doctor who had come to offer medical help, and threats to take a mentally disturbed suspect's wife into custody were ruled unconstitutional. The Court excluded not only confessions that were truly involuntary, but also those in which the police violated principles of fairness in dealing with suspects.

By 1960, the Court had developed a general standard of "voluntariness" in weighing confessions. Author John Taylor, a professor at Washington College, explained:

> In assessing the effect of police tactics on individual suspects, it looked to such factors as the age, intelligence, experience, and emotional stability of suspects and considered whether police had arrested and detained them legally, held them incommunicado, denied requests for counsel and access to friends, conducted extensive interrogation, resorted to intimidation, or employed trickery. No one factor was decisive . . . but the Court gradually placed more emphasis on police tactics (particularly prolonged interrogation) and less on the vulnerability of the suspect.[3]

At the time, the Court decided confession cases under the due process clause of the Fourteenth Amendment rather than under the Bill of Rights, the first 10 amendments to the Constitution. During the 1960s, however, the Court handed down a series of decision that made most of the protections of the Bill of Rights applicable to trials in state courts. (Appendix A in this book explains how the Court came to do so.)

Three decisions from that decade are crucial to the discussion about *Miranda* because they laid the groundwork for that decision. The first was *Gideon v. Wainwright*, in 1963. *Gideon* held that a defendant's Sixth Amendment's right to "have the Assistance of Counsel for his defence"[4] applied to state criminal trials. It also ruled that, if a defendant lacked funds to hire a lawyer, the court would appoint one at state expense.

Another landmark decision that led to *Miranda* was *Malloy v. Hogan*, in 1964, which held that the privilege against self-incrimination—to "incriminate" means to accuse oneself of a crime—applied to trials in state courts. That privilege is derived from the Fifth Amendment, which provides that "no person . . . shall be compelled in any criminal case to be a witness against himself."[5]

That same year, the Court decided *Escobedo v. Illinois*, a confession case that rested on the Sixth Amendment. In *Escobedo*, the Court held that the suspect's confession should not have been admitted because the police refused his request to talk to his lawyer while he was being questioned at the police station. By the time Ernesto Miranda's appeal came before the Arizona Supreme Court, *Escobedo* had become the law of the land. The Arizona justices read *Escobedo* narrowly, however: They concluded that the police had no obligation to tell a suspect that he had the right to a lawyer. Miranda's lawyers disagreed. They argued that the right to counsel was meaningless if an ignorant suspect—Miranda had only a grade-school education—was unaware that such a right existed.

The *Miranda* Decision

When they prepared their appeal to the Supreme Court, Ernesto Miranda's lawyers believed that it was a right-to-counsel case. By the time the case was argued, however, the justices had concluded that it was a self-incrimination case based on the Fifth Amendment, though the right to counsel played a role, as well.

On June 13, 1966, the Court ruled that the police violated Ernesto Miranda's rights. The vote was 5 to 4. Even though the police had used no physical or psychological coercion, the majority of justices believed that questioning inside a police station was, by its very nature, coercive:

> This atmosphere carries its own badge of intimidation. To be sure, this is not physical intimidation, but it is equally destructive of human dignity. The current practice of incommunicado interrogation is at odds with one of our Nation's most cherished principles—that the individual may not be compelled to incriminate himself.[6]

The *Miranda* Court pointed out that police departments had a history of using brutal tactics to extract confessions. They conceded that the use of the "third degree"—physical violence—was becoming a thing of the past, but they found that the police had begun to employ psychological tactics that were equally coercive:

Escobedo v. Illinois: The Last Stop on the Road to *Miranda*

On January 19, 1960, Manuel Valtierra was fatally shot. The police brought Valtierra's brother-in-law, Danny Escobedo, into custody. They knew that Benedict DiGerlando, who was already in custody, had admitted to firing the fatal shots, but they believed that Escobedo had plotted Valtierra's murder. Escobedo asked to see his lawyer but was refused. His lawyer went to the police station and was denied the opportunity to meet with his client.

One detective told Escobedo that DiGerlando had accused him of shooting Valtierra and asked him, "Would you care to tell DiGerlando that?" Escobedo replied, "Yes, I will." The detective brought Escobedo in to confront DiGerlando. He told DiGerlando that he was lying and said, "I didn't shoot Manuel, you did it."

Escobedo's statement was not a confession, but it was incriminating. For the first time, he admitted that he knew of the plot to kill Valtierra. In many interrogations, the suspect provides less than a full confession—a "full confession" includes an acknowledgment of guilt and a description of the facts of the crime—but tells the police enough to allow them to pursue other leads or fill gaps in the case. Escobedo's statement led to further questioning by the police and, finally, to a statement on which his indictment for murder was based.

Escobedo was convicted of murder. Eventually, that conviction was affirmed by the Supreme Court of Illinois. Escobedo appealed to the United States Supreme Court. He argued that the police had denied him his Sixth Amendment right to counsel.

In *Escobedo v. Illinois,* 378 U.S. 478 (1964), a five-member majority of the Court agreed with Danny Escobedo. Because the police had denied him his right to consult with his lawyer, it ruled that his statement should have been suppressed.

In essence, it is this: to be alone with the subject is essential to prevent distraction and to deprive him of any outside support. The aura of confidence in his guilt undermines his will to resist. He merely confirms the preconceived story the police seek to have him describe. Patience and persistence, at times relentless questioning, are employed.[7]

Justice Arthur Goldberg wrote the majority opinion.

The *Escobedo* case raised the question of when the right to counsel arose. Justice Goldberg proposed the following standard for when a suspect was entitled to consult with his lawyer: "Where … the investigation is no longer a general inquiry into an unsolved crime but has begun to focus on a particular suspect, the suspect has been taken into police custody, the police carry out a process of interrogations that lends itself to eliciting incriminating statements."

Justice Goldberg also raised a broader argument—namely, that a justice system that depended on confessions was less reliable and more prone to abuses than one that relied on independent evidence obtained through investigation. He added, "If the exercise of constitutional rights will thwart the effectiveness of a system of law enforcement, then there is something very wrong with that system."

Justice Potter Stewart, one of the four dissenters, maintained that the right to counsel should not apply until "formal prosecutorial proceedings" had started "by way of indictment, information, or arraignment." Justice Byron White accused the majority of imposing its idea of what constituted "civilized" police behavior. Justice White warned that the majority's focus-of-the-investigation test would be "wholly unworkable and impossible to administer unless police cars are equipped with public defenders and undercover agents and police informants have defense counsel at their side." He also charged that the majority had overstepped its authority to apply the Constitution and made decisions that should have been made by state legislatures.

Escobedo added to the uncertainty as to when a suspect's right to counsel arose and when the police were obligated to warn the suspect of his or her rights. The result was a flood of appeals by defendants who challenged their interrogation by the police. One of those appeals was Ernesto Miranda's.

The Court went on to state that "unless adequate protective devices are employed to dispel the compulsion inherent in custodial surroundings, no statement obtained from the defendant can truly be the product of his free choice."[8] It then spelled out the *Miranda* rule, which can be summarized as follows:

- The rule applies when a person either has been taken into custody or has been deprived of his freedom of action in any significant way.

- Before interrogating the suspect, the police must give him all four *Miranda* warnings: (1) He has a right to remain silent, (2) any statement he does make may be used as evidence against him, (3) he has a right to have a lawyer present, and (4) if he lacks the money to hire a lawyer, one will be appointed for him.

- The suspect may *waive*—that is, voluntarily give up—*Miranda* rights; however, the prosecution must show the court that the suspect "voluntarily, knowingly, and intelligently" did so.

- During interrogation, if the suspect tells the police that he wishes to consult with a lawyer or that he does not wish to be interrogated, the police must stop questioning him.

- If the police violate the *Miranda* rule, the prosecution may not use the suspect's statement as evidence.

Miranda's Aftermath

Miranda was strongly resented by the police, prosecutors, and millions of Americans, who already were concerned that crime had gotten out of control. On Capitol Hill, lawmakers explored ways to overturn *Miranda*. After weighing several alternatives, they added a new provision to the federal criminal code: Title 18,

Section 3501, of the United States Code, which would reinstate the pre-*Miranda* voluntariness standard. Supporters did not know it at the time, but §3501 would lay dormant for more than 30 years.

That same year saw a much more significant political event. Americans elected Richard Nixon, who promised to appoint "strict constructionists"—that is, judges who would apply the law as is and not create new rights—to the Supreme Court. In 1969, Nixon got his first opportunity to fill a Supreme Court vacancy when Chief Justice Earl Warren retired. His replacement was Warren Burger, a federal appeals court judge who had been highly critical of *Miranda*. During his presidency, Nixon filled three more vacancies. With four new justices and two of the four dissenters in the *Miranda* decision still on the Court, it appeared that *Miranda*'s days were numbered. That decision was never overturned, however. A major reason is that the Court has a strong tradition of *stare decisis*, a Latin phrase that means "let things decided stand." It is unusual for the Court to overturn an earlier decision outright, even if a majority disagrees with it. Instead, it limits the effect of such decisions by creating exceptions to them or by refusing to take them to their logical conclusion. The Burger Court did that to *Miranda*.

Harris v. New York, in 1971, was the first major court test for *Miranda*. The prosecution attempted to introduce a statement that the police obtained from the defendant, Viven Harris, in violation of the *Miranda* rule. At Harris's trial, the prosecution used portions of his statement to show the jury that he had told the police a different story. When the case was appealed, the Court held that it was permissible to use the statement to impeach—that is, cast doubt on—Harris's testimony.

After *Harris*, the Court handed down more decisions that not only weakened the *Miranda* rule, but indicated that the justices might eventually overturn *Miranda* itself. Conservatives believed that a test case involving §3501 would spell the end of *Miranda*. Because federal authorities were careful to follow *Miranda*, however, it took years for such a case to materialize. Finally, in 2000, one did. FBI agents investigating a bank robbery questioned Charles Dickerson, the suspected driver of the getaway car, without reading him his *Miranda* rights. The U.S. Court of Appeals for the Fourth Circuit concluded that his confession was "voluntary" within the meaning of §3501 and should be admitted. When the case was appealed, the Supreme Court agreed to take up the case.

The Supreme Court Reaffirms *Miranda*

To the surprise of many observers, the Court ruled in *Dickerson v. United States*, that *Miranda* was still the law. Chief Justice William Rehnquist, writing for a seven-member majority, stated,

> *Miranda* has become embedded in routine police practice to the point where the warnings have become part of our national culture. While we have overruled our precedents when subsequent cases have undermined their doctrinal underpinnings, we do not believe that this has happened to the *Miranda* decision.[9]

Most legal experts believe that the Court is unlikely to reconsider *Miranda* anytime soon. Nevertheless, *Dickerson* did not end the debate over *Miranda*. Advocates of law and order believe that the *Miranda* rule deprives the police of tens of thousands of confessions every year, leaving crimes unsolved and letting criminals remain at large. Judicial conservatives insist that there is no constitutional basis for the rule. Even civil libertarians are dissatisfied with *Miranda*. They maintain that the Court has watered it down over the years. The debate took on a new dimension in light of the September 11, 2001, terrorist attacks. These attacks led many Americans to reconsider the balance between respect for individual rights and the public's right to be secure.

Summary

Miranda v. Arizona is one of the Supreme Court's best-known and most controversial decisions. In *Miranda*, the Court applied both the Fifth Amendment right not to incriminate oneself and the Sixth Amendment right to the assistance of legal counsel to interrogations by the police. In addition, the Court imposed a four-part rule that the police must follow when they question a suspect in custody. *Miranda* was the last major criminal law decision of the Warren Court. Although the Court has become more conservative, it reaffirmed *Miranda* in 2000. It is widely believed that *Miranda* has become a permanent part of American law; however, the ruling continues to be heavily criticized.

Miranda Was Wrongly Decided and Should Be Overruled

B y the time it decided *Miranda*, the Supreme Court had become so unpopular that "Impeach Earl Warren" billboards were a common sight in many parts of country. Many Americans were of the view that the nine unelected justices injected their personal views about fairness into the Constitution. As journalist Liva Baker observed:

> The justices had become increasingly cantankerous, upsetting long-established customs and altering long-established procedures, all in the name of upholding the constitutional rights of the individual. They had interfered in the operation of the public schools of the nation, declaring racial segregation unconstitutional there. They had meddled in local politics, attacking malapportioned voting districts. They had tampered with the operations of government, interfering

with the ways officials could deal with citizens who espoused unpopular ideas and with the way police could deal with the criminal defendants.[10]

Today, many Americans still consider *Miranda* a symbol of judges who "legislate from the bench."

There is no constitutional basis for the *Miranda* rule.

Justice Antonin Scalia, who believed that *Miranda* should have been overruled, dissented in *Dickerson v. United States*, the ruling that reaffirmed *Miranda*. He wrote, "What today's decision will stand for, whether the Justices can bring themselves to say it or not, is the power of the Supreme Court to write a prophylactic, extraconstitutional Constitution, binding on Congress and the States."[11] Justice Scalia and other "strict constructionists" argue that *Miranda* expanded on what the legal community had long considered the intended scope of the Fifth Amendment.

The privilege against self-incrimination, on which the Fifth Amendment is based, was first recognized by early British courts. Lawyer and author Robert Precht explains,

> Initially, it was a reaction to the practices of royal inquisitors of hauling people before tribunals without telling them the evidence against them and of requiring the accused to explain themselves in the hopes of uncovering incriminating information. This procedure was frequently accompanied by torture. Because of the citizenry's strong revulsion at the abuse of royal prerogatives, English jurisprudence developed a broad rule—some commentators believe too broad—that it was illegal to force anyone to explain himself, whether he was told the evidence against him or not. The rule survives today, even though the original impetus for the rule—requiring a person to appear in court without detailed charges—has ceased.[12]

Justice Byron White, who dissented in *Miranda*, emphasized that the privilege against self-incrimination applied to questioning in the courtroom, not the police station:

> The privilege, firmly established in the second half of the seventeenth century, was never applied except to prohibit compelled judicial interrogations.
>
> The rule excluding coerced confessions matured about 100 years later, [but] . . . the privilege, as such, seems to have been given effect only in judicial proceedings, including the preliminary examinations by authorized magistrates.[13]

Critics of *Miranda* maintain that the Court also erred by extending the Sixth Amendment: Originally, the right to counsel applied to the courtroom only, not to questioning elsewhere. In *Escobedo v. Illinois*, Justice Potter Stewart argued in dissent, "Under our system of criminal justice, the institution of formal, meaningful judicial proceedings, by way of indictment, information, or arraignment, marks the point at which a criminal investigation has ended and adversary proceedings have commenced."[14] Eight years later, in 1972, the Court agreed with Justice Stewart. In *Kirby v. Illinois*, it held that the right to counsel did not arise until the defendant was formally charged with a crime. Nevertheless, the *Miranda* rule, which entitles a suspect to have a lawyer present during questioning at the police station, remains part of American law.

Finally, opponents of *Miranda* argue that the Court expanded the concept of "coercion" far beyond what the Framers of the Constitution had intended. The Framers were concerned with the use of torture and threats of criminal or civil penalties to pressure suspects to admit guilt. With *Lisenba v. California* in 1941, however, the Court began to disallow confessions on the grounds that police tactics violated fundamental notions of fairness, not because they were coerced and therefore unreliable. Twenty-five years later, the *Miranda*

Court did away with the need to prove coercion when it found that in-custody interrogation was by its very nature coercive. In Ernesto Miranda's case, the interrogation lasted only two hours and the police did not resort to physical force or psychological manipulation to pressure him to confess. The only coercion in that case, critics contend, was that which the Court had invented.

Critics believed that the Warren Court had come to the conclusion that such interrogation was "uncivilized" and was moving to abolish it. As Justice White observed in *Escobedo*, the majority's decision was "another major step in the direction of the goal which the Court seemingly has in mind—to bar from evidence all admissions obtained from an individual suspected of crime, whether involuntarily made or not."[15]

Legislatures, not courts, should write rules of criminal procedure.

Critics of *Miranda* and other Warren Court decisions argued that the Framers would be shocked to discover that the federal courts had transformed the Constitution into a code of criminal procedure. They did not object to the Court's reviewing criminal convictions and remedying miscarriages of justice—resolving individual cases is what courts do best—but thought that imposing standards such as the *Miranda* rule was inappropriate. Journalist Liva Baker summarized the critics' argument: "The judiciary, which could stop only what was wrong, was ill-equipped to set down what was right; detailed instructions to the law enforcement community was a legislative, not a judicial, function."[16] *Miranda*'s critics add that judges are especially unqualified to supervise police work because they rarely have firsthand experience with it. As Warren Burger remarked before he joined the Court, "The resolution of great issues . . . deserved the careful attention of expert participants in the field, not Supreme Court justices writing in isolation from events—the broad-based support of the state legislatures."[17]

Miranda thwarts the will of the people.

In his dissenting opinion in _Dickerson_, Justice Scalia also accused the _Miranda_ and _Dickerson_ Courts of having seized power that rightfully belonged to the people. He wrote:

> I see little harm in admitting that we made a mistake in taking away from the people the ability to decide for themselves what

The Exclusionary Rule

If the police violate a suspect's constitutional rights, what can the courts do about it? The Supreme Court has wrestled with this question for years, especially in cases in which the police had unlawfully searched a person or his or her home. Since 1914, it has applied the _exclusionary rule_, under which the prosecution cannot use evidence in court that it was obtained illegally.

Weeks v. United States, 232 U.S. 383 (1914), was a case in which federal agents entered the home of a man, Fremont Weeks, without a search warrant and found evidence that he was sending lottery tickets by mail (a violation of federal law). Weeks appealed his conviction, arguing that the search of his home violated the Fourth Amendment. The Court agreed with him. In doing so, it explained the purpose of the exclusionary rule:

> If letters and private documents can thus be seized and held and used in evidence against a citizen accused of an offense, the protection of the Fourth Amendment declaring his right to be secure against such searches and seizures, is of no value, and, so far as those thus placed are concerned, might as well be stricken from the Constitution....
>
> To sanction such proceedings would be to affirm by judicial decision a manifest neglect, if not an open defiance, of the prohibitions of the Constitution, intended for the protection of the people against such unauthorized action.[*]

Until 1961, the exclusionary rule laid down by _Weeks_ applied to federal, but not state, criminal prosecutions. In _Mapp v. Ohio_, 367 U.S. 643 (1961), the Supreme Court reversed itself and made the exclusionary rule applicable to all criminal cases. The _Mapp_ case began when police officers broke into Dorlee Mapp's home and found obscene materials inside. Mapp appealed her obscenity conviction to the Supreme Court, which reversed it. In applying the exclusionary rule, which the Ohio courts did not then recognize, the Court stated:

protections (beyond those required by the Constitution) are reasonably affordable in the criminal investigatory process. And I see much to be gained by reaffirming for the people the wonderful reality that they govern themselves.[18]

Others critics argue that, whether or not *Miranda* was a proper interpretation of the Constitution, the Court had unwisely

And nothing could be more certain than that, when a coerced confession is involved, "the relevant rules of evidence" are overridden without regard to "the incidence of such conduct by the police," slight or frequent. Why should not the same rule apply to what is tantamount to coerced testimony by way of unconstitutional seizure of goods, papers, effects, documents, etc.?[**]

The exclusionary rule has been at the center of controversy for years. Opponents contend that it prevents juries from learning the truth and allows guilty defendants to go free, often because of a minor error by a police officer. They often quote Justice Benjamin Cardozo's famous observation, "The criminal is to go free because the constable has blundered."[***] Supporters of the rule argue that the alternatives to excluding unlawfully obtained evidence do not discourage the police from breaking the law. In fact, the *Mapp* Court responded to Cardozo, "The criminal goes free, if he must, but it is the law that sets him free. Nothing can destroy a government more quickly than its failure to observe its own laws, or worse, its disregard of the charter of its own existence."[†]

One question presented to the Court was how far the exclusionary rule extended. In *Wong Sun v. United States*, 371 U.S. 471 (1963), it adopted the "fruit of the poisonous tree" doctrine. In *Wong Sun*, evidence seized in violation of the Fourth Amendment led federal agents to evidence of another crime. The defendant in the second crime argued that the evidence should not be used against him because it was the result of the original unlawful search. The Court agreed with him. It characterized the evidence as the poisoned "fruit" of the original constitutional violation. Even though the "fruit of the poisonous tree" doctrine applies in Fourth Amendment cases, the Supreme Court held in *Michigan v. Tucker*, 417 U.S. 433 (1974), that it does not apply to the "fruits" of a violation of the *Miranda* rule.

[*]232 U.S. 393, 393–394
[**]367 U.S. 643, 656
[***]*People v. Defore*, 242 N.Y. 13, 21, 150 N.E. 585, 587 (1926)
[†]367 U.S. 643, 656

The U.S. Supreme Court building (above) in Washington, D.C., houses the highest court in the land. The Supreme Court almost exclusively hears cases that have gone through many levels of state and federal appeals courts.

exercised its power. During the oral arguments of *Miranda*, prosecutors contended that the states were better qualified to determine what rules should apply to custodial interrogation. They also told the Court that requiring the police to warn suspects of the right to remain silent and to have a lawyer present was out of step with current practice in the states. Justice John Harlan made that point in his *Miranda* dissent, noting that a majority of states had submitted legal briefs opposing the *Miranda* rule, whereas no states had submitted a brief in support.

In contrast, states had supported some of the Court's other decisions: More than half the states had adopted some form of the exclusionary rule when the Court decided *Mapp v. Ohio* in 1961, and 22 of the 24 states that submitted briefs to the Court in *Gideon v. Wainwright* in 1963 supported a national requirement that courts appoint lawyers for felony defendants who lacked the funds to hire one on their own. The Court's unwillingness to listen to the people and their elected lawmakers can lead to a political backlash. In recent years, decisions that involve flag-burning, expression of religion, and the death penalty have proved so controversial that some members of Congress reacted by introducing legislation that would strip the Court of jurisdiction over certain cases.

Finally, opponents of *Miranda* accuse the Court of having too little faith in the criminal justice system, especially the police. As lawyer and author Gary Stuart observed, "The *Miranda* decision [was] unique in its message—sent to the world at large—that police officers are not to be trusted."[19]

Critics of *Miranda* point out that there are number of checks on rogue police officers: Prosecutors have an ethical obligation to see that justice is done and, in any event, want to avoid the embarrassment of arguing a trumped-up case. Appeals courts can reverse miscarriages of justice that occur at the trial stage and earlier. Abusive police officers run the risk of civil lawsuits and, in extreme cases, can face criminal charges: Some of the police officers who tortured Abner Louima inside a New York City stationhouse were later charged with serious crimes, and a jury awarded Louima nearly $6 million in his lawsuit against the police department. The possibility of bad publicity also discourages the police from breaking the law. Every police officer is aware that the beating of motorist Rodney King became a worldwide news story because a bystander with a video camera happened to record it.

Perhaps most important, juries serve as a check on police misconduct. Paul Cassell, a professor at the University of Utah and a vocal opponent of *Miranda*, wrote:

> The kinds of issues swirling around false confessions seem readily susceptible to jury evaluation. Did the suspect confess to details only the real perpetrator would know? Did the cops "feed" the information to the suspect? Is there some innocent

Trial Courts, Appeals, and Appellate Review

Court systems in the United States are divided into two levels. The lower level consists of *trial courts*, whose function is to decide the facts of the case and apply the law. Most cases are tried before a jury, which listens to witnesses and decides whose story is more believable. Jurors also evaluate demonstrative evidence such as weapons, crime scene photographs, and the results of blood work and other tests. They decide how much weight to give this evidence, as well. Those evaluations lead to the jury's ultimate decision—whether the defendant is guilty or innocent.

The upper level consists of *appellate courts*, whose function is to correct errors made by trial courts. Appellate judges do not substitute their own view of the facts for that of the jury, for the simple reason that the jurors saw the evidence firsthand and the appellate judges do not. Their focus is on legal errors, such as violations of the rules of evidence. An appellate court will not reverse a judgment unless the lower court committed legal errors that were serious enough to change the outcome of the trial.

In criminal cases, the vast majority of appeals are brought by convicted defendants. That is so because the Constitution's prohibition of double jeopardy bars the prosecution from appealing a not-guilty verdict. Under some circumstances, though, the prosecution may appeal a judge's pretrial ruling. That happened in *Dickerson v. United States*, 530 U.S. 428 (2000), the case that reaffirmed *Miranda*.

The federal system and most states have two levels of appeals courts, typically called the "Court of Appeals" and the "Supreme Court." A defendant is usually entitled to appeal a conviction to the next higher court. Appeals after the first one are *discretionary*. In other words, a higher court will hear the case only if it raises serious legal questions that it believes need to be resolved.

With rare exceptions, the Supreme Court does not have to hear a case. Every year, the Court receives about 7,500 petitions, many of them from prisoners like Ernesto Miranda, asking for a *writ of certiorari*. Certiorari is an order by the Supreme Court that directs the lower court to send up the record of a case so that it can be reviewed for legal errors.

The Court grants certiorari in only a fraction of cases that come before it—usually 80 to 160 per year. In general, a party that asks for certiorari must meet three criteria. First, he or she must have exhausted appeals in the state court system. Second, his or her claim must be that the state courts denied him or her rights under the Constitution or an act of Congress. Finally, at least four of the nine justices must consider the issues raised important enough for the Court to review. Although the decision as to which cases are "certworthy" is subjective, the four-vote rule is rigidly followed. Many people believe that a refusal to grant certiorari implies agreement with the ruling being appealed. A denial of certiorari is not an expression of opinion, however, but rather is the Court's determination that an issue is not worth deciding, is better resolved by the lower courts, or is not yet appropriate to take up.

explanation for the incriminating statement from the suspect? These are not subjects generally beyond the ken of the average jury.[20]

Police practices would have improved without *Miranda.*

In his dissenting opinion, Justice Harlan expressed concern that the *Miranda* rule would curtail efforts to develop effective—and politically more acceptable—alternatives. He wrote:

> Of course legislative reform is rarely speedy or unanimous, though this Court has been more patient in the past. But the legislative reforms when they come would have the vast advantage of empirical data and comprehensive study, they would allow experimentation and use of solutions not open to the courts, and they would restore the initiative in criminal law reform to those forums where it truly belongs.[21]

At the time the justices were considering *Miranda*, the American Law Institute (ALI) was drafting a Model Code of Pre-Arraignment Procedure that would set standards for govern interrogation. The ALI's proposal incorporated some, but not all, of the *Miranda* rule. Although the Model Code had no legal effect of its own, the work of the ALI has been very influential on state courts and legislatures. In fact, states already were beginning to adopt rules to govern the interrogation of suspects. Liva Baker observed that, during the 1960s, "the general direction of state legislation was to provide counsel at ever-earlier stages; the discrepancies between the quality of justice meted out inside the station house and the courtroom were beginning to diminish."[22] It can be argued that, had the Court not interfered, many states might have required some version of the *Miranda* rule on their own and would have been free to correct flaws in the rule. Instead, the states and the police are saddled with a rigid standard that is now more than 40 years old.

Finally, many in the criminal justice field maintain that the quality of police departments has improved substantially

Miranda's Companion Cases

Many Americans are familiar with the *Miranda* case itself, but few are aware of the three "companion cases" that the Supreme Court decided with *Miranda*. It is not uncommon for the Court to decide a number of cases that raise similar legal issues together. *Brown v. Board of Education* (1954), the landmark school desegregation decision, and *Roe v. Wade* (1973), which swept aside most state restrictions on abortion, were each decided along with companion cases.

At the beginning of its 1965–1966 term, the Court had received dozens of petitions from defendants who argued that their confessions had been obtained in violation of the Constitution. The justices chose *Miranda* and its companion cases carefully. They were looking for cases that did not involve inflammatory aspects such as a child victim, had no side issues to cloud the question of whether the defendant's confession was obtained lawfully, and represented a diverse group of states and a variety of offenses. The justices ultimately chose the following:

- No. 760, *Vignera v. New York*. Michael Vignera was picked up by New York police on suspicion of robbery. At the trial, the defense lawyer asked the detective who interrogated Vignera whether he had advised Vignera of his right to counsel before questioning began. The judge refused to allow the detective to answer. There was nothing in the record to show that Vignera was warned of his rights before he was questioned or that the authorities had taken any other steps to protect those rights.

- No. 761, *Westover v. United States*. Carl Westover was arrested by Kansas City police in connection with two robberies. There was nothing in the record to indicate that the police advised him of his rights. They questioned him for hours without obtaining a confession and then turned him over to FBI agents, who suspected him of two bank robberies in California. The FBI agents advised Westover of his rights, but he confessed to the bank robberies anyway. He was later convicted in federal court.

since the *Miranda* Court criticized them. They point out that departments have more funding, officers are better educated and trained, and technology has made it possible to build a case against a defendant on the basis of independently gathered

Westover's lawyers argued that their client had in effect undergone one continuous interrogation conducted by different police officers and that he should have been warned before questioning began.

- No. 584, *California v. Stewart*. Roy Stewart was arrested by Los Angeles police in connection with a robbery in which the victim later died. The police held him for five days, during which time they questioned him nine different times. At the trial, the police officers could not recall whether they had advised Stewart of his rights. The Supreme Court of California reversed Stewart's conviction because it found nothing in the record to indicate that he had been advised of his rights or that he had knowingly and intelligently waived them. California appealed, arguing that the state supreme court had misinterpreted the United States Constitution.

Miranda and its companion cases all raised similar issues: The defendant was questioned by the authorities while in custody, he was not fully advised of his rights when questioning began, and he confessed to the crime and was later convicted.

There nearly was a fourth companion case to *Miranda*. It was an appeal by Sylvester Johnson and Stanley Cassidy, who had been convicted of murder in New Jersey. Although that case was argued with *Miranda*, the Court decided it separately in order to address the issue of *retroactivity*—that is, whether a decision should benefit defendants who had already been convicted. The Court rarely gives decisions retroactive effect because doing so could disrupt the criminal justice system. The Court concluded that failing to warn a suspect of the right to remain silent and to consult with a lawyer was not a serious enough violation to justify making *Miranda* retroactive. Accordingly, in *Johnson v. New Jersey* (1966), it held that *Miranda* would apply only to cases in which the defendant's trial began on or after June 13, 1966, the day that decision was announced.

evidence rather than obtaining evidence in the form of the defendant's own words.

Summary

Many people think that *Miranda* was bad law when it was first decided and remains bad law today. In deciding *Miranda*, the Supreme Court asserted power that the Constitution had not given it. The Court also expanded the Fifth Amendment privilege against self-incrimination and the Sixth Amendment right to counsel beyond what the Framers of the Constitution had intended. *Miranda* was bad policy as well as bad law: It imposed a rigid rule that prevented state and local governments from developing approaches that might have better served the interests of both suspected criminals and the public.

Miranda Is Consistent With the Bill of Rights

Having seen King George III's abuses of power firsthand, the Framers were determined to make sure that such abuses did not happen again. As author Gary Stuart observed:

> The first ten amendments to the Constitution have been crucial to the development of the political and legal systems of the United States. Collectively, they portray an important ideal: that the people have rights, which no government may withhold. It was for the express purpose of preventing tyrants from restricting the rights of citizens that the framers of the Constitution embedded this ideal and also pragmatically provided the basis for actually securing the rights they envisioned.[23]

Nearly two centuries later, the Supreme Court handed down *Miranda v. Arizona*. Many Americans believed that the *Miranda*

Court had overstepped its power, but Richard Leo, a professor at the University of California, Irvine, and a *Miranda* supporter, disagrees. He wrote, "Although the Warren Court appeared to fashion the *Miranda* warnings from whole cloth, the privilege against compelled self-incrimination has enjoyed a long history in Anglo-American law as a bulwark against oppressive state questioning."[24]

Police misconduct is a long-standing problem.

Miranda was not a spur-of-the-moment decision. For years, it was known that the police had mistreated suspects, often brutally. The *Miranda* Court alluded to the Wickersham Report, in which a presidential commission found widespread use of the "third degree" to extract confessions from suspects. Liva Baker explained:

> Commission investigators had documented hundreds of examples of beatings, pistol whippings, strappings, lynching threats, solitary confinement in rat-infested jail cells, application of the "water cure"—holding a suspect's head under water for long periods—and protracted questioning, all in order to elicit confessions for offenses that ranged from murder to stealing a hog.[25]

The Wickersham Report was made public in 1931. Although physical coercion had become less common by the time *Miranda* was decided, the Court pointed out that the police had become skilled at using psychological coercion. It quoted from police manuals that set out interrogation techniques, and then stated:

> From these representative samples of interrogation techniques, the setting prescribed by the manuals and observed in practice becomes clear. . . . The aura of confidence in his guilt undermines his will to resist. He merely confirms the preconceived story the police seek to have him describe. . . . When normal procedures fail to produce the needed result, the police may resort to deceptive stratagems such as giving

false legal advice. It is important to keep the subject off balance, for example, by trading on his insecurity about himself or his surroundings. The police then persuade, trick, or cajole him out of exercising his constitutional rights.[26]

Thirty years after *Brown v. Mississippi*, the first state-level case in which the Court overturned a conviction because the defendant's confession was coerced, the Court stated that the police were still taking advantage of suspects inside the stationhouse. In *Miranda*, it told the police, "enough."

The *Miranda* rule makes important rights meaningful.

The Bill of Rights is worth little without some means to enforce it. In our system, that task falls on the judicial branch. American courts have the power of *judicial review*—that is, they can declare the actions of other branches of government unconstitutional.

The *Miranda* decision was an effort to enforce two key provisions of the Bill of Rights. The first of these is the Sixth Amendment right to counsel, which helps protect the innocent from being found guilty of a crime. In *Powell v. Alabama*, the Court recognized the importance of the "guiding hand of counsel," writing,

> Left without the aid of counsel he may be put on trial without a proper charge, and convicted upon incompetent evidence, or evidence irrelevant to the issue or otherwise inadmissible. He lacks both the skill and knowledge adequately to prepare his defense, even though he have a perfect one.[27]

The other constitutional right protected by the *Miranda* rule is the Fifth Amendment's privilege against self-incrimination. The Anglo-American legal system is "accusatorial" in nature, which means that the state must prove the accused's guilt of the crime—often described as "innocent until proven guilty." This is in contrast to "inquisitorial" systems, in which judges ask the questions and the accused is faced with a no-win situation: He or she can admit guilt, lie to the judge and risk the consequences, or face punishment for contempt of court if he or she refuses to talk. *Miranda* addressed what amounted to inquisitorial proceedings conducted by the police.

A Twentieth-Century Case of Torture: *Brown v. Mississippi*

More than 300 years after the English Parliament abolished the Court of Star Chamber, a secret court that had the power to inflict physical punishment (short of death) on defendants, the United States Supreme Court found itself confronted by a twentieth-century case of torture. That case, *Brown v. Mississippi*, 297 U.S. 46 (1936), played a significant role in shaping the law of confessions and helped make the *Miranda* decision possible.

The case began when a deputy sheriff and a number of white men seized an African-American sharecropper named Arthur Ellington. They whipped him mercilessly and afterward warned him that the whippings would continue until he confessed to the murder of a white man named Raymond Stewart. The same deputy, accompanied by other white men, later took sharecroppers Ed Brown and Henry Shields into custody and whipped both men until their backs were cut to pieces. They, too, were warned that the whippings would continue until they not only confessed, but did so in the exact words demanded. All three men were further warned that, if they tried to tell a different story than what they were told, they would face further punishment.

All three men did what they were told and formally confessed to the murder. At their trial, the prosecution argued that the confessions were voluntary. The confessions were the only evidence against them. The deputy sheriff who extracted the confessions admitted that he had tortured the defendants, and two other men admitted their role in the whippings. No one denied what happened.

The jury found the men guilty, and they were sentenced to death. The Supreme Court of Mississippi affirmed the convictions, holding that the defense lawyer failed to object to the admission of the confessions at the proper moment and, in any event, that compelling a person to incriminate himself was not necessarily a violation of Mississippi's constitution.

The U.S. Supreme Court unanimously reversed the convictions. Chief Justice Charles Evans Hughes wrote the majority opinion. He remarked, "It is sufficient to

The *Miranda* rule promotes fairer trials.

Criminal trials are governed by rules aimed at excluding unreliable evidence. For example, expert witnesses must show that they have specialized knowledge to offer the jury, hearsay

say that in pertinent respects the transcript reads more like pages torn from some medieval account than a record made within the confines of a modern civilization which aspires to an enlightened constitutional government." He also quoted from an earlier opinion of the Supreme Court of Mississippi, which stated that the practice of coercing confessions "has been the curse of all countries [and] was the chief iniquity, the crowning infamy of the Star Chamber, and the Inquisition, and other similar institutions."

The chief justice concluded that "compulsion by torture to extort a confession" was a denial of due process of law. In doing so, he stressed that there were limits to states' power to punish crimes:

> The State is free to regulate the procedure of its courts in accordance with its own conceptions of policy, unless in so doing it "offends some principle of justice so rooted in the traditions and conscience of our people as to be ranked as fundamental." . . . The rack and torture chamber may not be substituted for the witness stand. The state may not permit an accused to be hurried to conviction under mob domination—where the whole proceeding is but a mask—without supplying corrective process. . . . It would be difficult to conceive of methods more revolting to the sense of justice than those taken to procure the confessions of these petitioners, and the use of the confessions thus obtained as the basis for conviction and sentence was a clear denial of due process.

He then concluded that the Mississippi courts should not have denied the defense motion to exclude the confessions on what amounted to a technicality. He wrote, "[The defendants'] complaint is not of the commission of mere error, but of a wrong so fundamental that it made the whole proceeding a mere pretense of a trial and rendered the conviction and sentence wholly void."

Unfortunately for Ed Brown and his two codefendants, the case did not end there. Despite the lack of evidence against them, they pled guilty to manslaughter and spent years in prison.

evidence—statements made by someone who cannot be brought into court—is generally not admitted, and the whereabouts of physical evidence, such as bloodstains, must be accounted for from the time it is collected. Likewise, judges have long known about the unreliability of coerced confessions. In *King v. Warickshall* in 1783, an English judge wrote:

> A free and voluntary confession is deserving of the highest credit, because it is presumed to flow from the strongest sense of guilt . . . but a confession forced from the mind by the flattery of hope, or by the torture of fear, comes in so questionable a shape . . . that no credit ought to be given to it; and therefore it is rejected.[28]

Coerced confessions are as unreliable today as they were in 1783, and the *Miranda* rule is an effort to prevent them.

It can also be argued that the *Miranda* rule was an effort to make trials meaningful. Yale Kamisar, a law professor at the University of Michigan and a *Miranda* supporter, has argued that two different justice systems, with different rules, exist in America. Kamisar believes that constitutional rights are often lost for good inside the "gatehouse," or police interrogation room. Gary Stuart explained:

> The gatehouse is where, in the pre-*Miranda* era, suspects talked, one way or the other. Of course, the conversation was private, no lawyers allowed. What the suspect said was typed up by the police and handed to the prosecutor. The prosecutor in turn carried the conversation, now labeled a "confession," up to the courthouse, which was often a majestic building where former suspects—now full-fledged defendants—became public persons. Now all those freshly typed words were read into the record. At least that was the case for the minority of suspects who insisted on a trial. The majority of unwarned suspects, when confronted privately with their confessions, adopted a much more efficient resolution: They pled guilty.[29]

Miranda has often been described as the next logical step after *Escobedo v. Illinois*. Both cases recognized what is at stake when a person is in police custody and the police have begun to question him or her. As the Court stated in *Escobedo*, "It would exalt form over substance to make the right to counsel, under these circumstances, depend on whether at the time of the interrogation, the authorities had secured a formal indictment. Petitioner had, for all practical purposes, already been charged with murder."[30]

When Danny Escobedo told Benedict DiGerlando, "I didn't shoot Manuel, you did it," in the presence of detectives, he thought he had cleared himself. That statement incriminated him as an accomplice to a murder, however. Under Illinois law, an accomplice was considered as much at fault as the person who actually killed the victim. Escobedo did not know that, but his lawyer certainly would have.

Before *Miranda*, a "sporting theory" of justice prevailed. Whether a suspect exercised his constitutional rights depended on whether he was aware of them. John Frank, a member of Ernesto Miranda's legal team, found that unacceptable. He argued, "The Constitution should not be kept secret from anyone, but especially from those who cannot read well enough to inform themselves."[31]

Ernesto Miranda's lawyers urged the Court to guarantee every criminal suspect, rich or poor, the right to counsel at a stage of the criminal process where important rights often were lost. In their brief to the Court, they argued, "We invoke the basic principles of *Powell v. Alabama*: 'He requires the guiding hand of counsel at every stop in the proceedings against him.' When [Ernesto] Miranda stepped into Interrogation Room 2, he had only the guiding hand of Officers Cooley and Young."[32] The Court agreed with Miranda's legal team. As Chief Justice Earl Warren wrote in his memoirs about that decision:

> It was of no assistance to hardened underworld types because they already know what their rights are and demand them. And it is so with all sophisticated criminals and affluent

prisoners who had ready access to their lawyers. However, because so many people who are arrested are poor and illiterate, short-cut methods and often cruelties are perpetrated to obtain convictions.[33]

FROM THE BENCH

The Case of the "Scottsboro Boys"

One of the most famous criminal trials of the twentieth century was that of the "Scottsboro Boys," nine young, illiterate African-American men who were convicted of rape in what is widely considered a miscarriage of justice.

The case began on March 25, 1931, when a sheriff's posse met a freight train outside Scottsboro, Alabama. They had received word that two young white women riding on the train had accused the young men of sexually assaulting them.

The defendants were quickly brought to trial. Soldiers guarded the courthouse, and the atmosphere outside was described as one of "tense, hostile, and excited public sentiment." The trial judge apparently never asked the defendants—who were from out of state—whether they wanted a lawyer appointed or whether relatives or friends back home could arrange for one. They were eventually represented by Milo Moody, a local lawyer, and Stephen Roddy, a Tennessee lawyer who was unfamiliar with Alabama law. Roddy, who handled most of the defense, had less than half an hour to meet with his clients before the trial.

The nine defendants were tried in assembly-line fashion, and eight were convicted (the ninth case ended in a mistrial). All eight were sentenced to death in the electric chair. Later, Alabama's highest court affirmed seven of the eight convictions. By this time, the case had gained national attention and the defendants were represented by new lawyers, who appealed to the Supreme Court. They argued on appeal that their clients had been denied due process of law because they did not receive a fair trial, were denied the right to counsel, and were not tried by a jury of their peers because African Americans were excluded.

In *Powell v. Alabama,* 287 U.S. 45 (1932), the Supreme Court reversed the convictions. The vote was 7 to 2. Justice George Sutherland, considered one of the Court's more conservative members, wrote the majority opinion. His opinion rested on only one of the three grounds for appeal—namely, the lack of legal representation at their trials. Justice Sutherland noted that the trial judge did not actually name Moody and Roddy as their lawyers until the very morning of the trial, the lawyers did not have an opportunity to investigate the facts, and their appearance was "rather pro forma rather than zealous and active."

Alternatives to *Miranda* are ineffective.
Opponents of *Miranda* insist that the pre-*Miranda* "voluntariness" standard should have been left in place. Solicitor General

Although Alabama's constitution did not entitle a criminal defendant to a lawyer, Justice Sutherland concluded that denying these defendants proper legal representation was a violation of due process of law. He explained the importance of having a lawyer at trial:

> Even the intelligent and educated layman has small and sometimes no skill in the science of law. . . . He requires the guiding hand of counsel at every step in the proceedings against him. Without it, though he be not guilty, he faces the danger of conviction because he does not know how to establish his innocence. If that be true of men of intelligence, how much more true is it of the ignorant and illiterate, or those of feeble intellect.

The right to counsel recognized by the *Powell* Court was limited. Justice Sutherland wrote:

> All that it is necessary now to decide, as we do decide, is that in a capital case, where the defendant is unable to employ counsel, and is incapable adequately of making his own defense because of ignorance, feeble-mindedness, illiteracy, or the like, it is the duty of the court, whether requested or not, to assign counsel for him as a necessary requisite of due process of law.

Justice Pierce Butler dissented. He contended that the defendants had in fact received adequate representation at their trial. He also argued that the defense had conducted "a very rigorous and rigid cross-examination" of the accusers and had filed motions to move the trial out of Scottsboro and to drop charges against two defendants on the grounds that they were juveniles.

The story of the Scottsboro Boys did not end with *Powell*. They were retried and convicted again. The Supreme Court reversed two of the convictions on retrial, holding in *Norris v. Alabama* (1935), and *Patterson v. Alabama* (1935), that the defendants had been denied due process of law because members of their race had been systematically excluded from the jury. Although none of the defendants were executed, they did serve varying amounts of prison time before dying, escaping, or serving their sentences. In October 1976, the last of the Scottsboro Boys, Clarence Norris, left prison after he was pardoned by Governor George Wallace.

Seth Waxman responded to that contention when *Dickerson v. United States* was argued to the Court:

> One, stability in the law, always important, was nowhere more important than in [*Miranda*], given the Court's dissatisfaction with the ambiguities of the totality-of-circumstances rules, as opposed to the certainty that *Miranda* provided. Two, *Miranda* had proven workable, its benefits to the administration of justice repeatedly emphasized and documented by the Supreme Court. Three, in all of its post-*Miranda* cases, the Supreme Court had affirmed *Miranda*'s underlying premise, that custodial interrogation created inherently compelling pressures and thus required some safeguards. And four, any re-evaluation of *Miranda* must take account of the Court's "profoundly unhappy experience," which had impelled it to adopt *Miranda* in the first place. In thirty-six cases over thirty years before 1965, the Court had simply been unable to articulate manageable totality-of-circumstances rules for the lower courts to apply.[34]

Miranda's supporters consider a clearly stated rule a better approach than an open-ended standard that was enforced after the fact in a relative handful of cases of serious police misconduct.

Opponents of *Miranda* also object to its use of the exclusionary rule—excluding statements that were obtained in violation of *Miranda*'s requirements. Justice Tom Clark, who wrote the decision that extended the exclusionary rule to the states in search and seizure cases, offered the following reply: "There are those who say that . . . 'the criminal is to go free because the constable has blundered.' . . . In some cases this will undoubtedly be the result. . . . The criminal goes free if he must, but it is the law that sets him free. Nothing can destroy government more quickly than its failure to observe its own laws."[35] Although the exclusionary rule is relatively new, it is rooted in an ancient principle that dates back to the Magna Carta: No person, not even the king, is above the law.

It has also been argued that the exclusionary rule is unnecessary because a defendant can later sue the police officers who violated his or her constitutional rights. The 2003 case of *Chavez v. Martinez* illustrates how difficult it is to win such a lawsuit. While receiving treatment for serious injuries in the hospital, Olivero Martinez was questioned persistently by a police officer. At least two justices of the Court suggested that the officer's actions could be seen as torture. The majority concluded that Martinez could not sue the officer for violating his Fifth Amendment rights, however, because Martinez was never charged with a crime. Martinez's case is unusual, not only because of its facts but also because Martinez won in the lower courts. It is difficult to win a lawsuit against police officers perceived to be "doing their job." The difficulty is compounded in interrogation cases, which tend to boil down to a one-sided "swearing contest" between the suspect and the police.

Summary

Miranda is consistent with the Bill of Rights and with centuries of Anglo-American legal tradition. Courts have long recognized that compelling a person accused of a crime to accuse him- or herself leads to unreliable evidence and violates his or her dignity. The *Miranda* Court was aware that, for years, the police had used coercion—psychological as well as physical—to extract confessions from suspects. The justices believed that the pre-*Miranda* voluntariness standard was ineffective and that stronger measures were needed to stop coercion in the stationhouse. For that reason, they imposed the *Miranda* rule on the nation's police.

Given Today's Crime Problem, *Miranda* Is Inappropriate

Nearly everyone has heard some variation of the "ticking time bomb" scenario: The police have a member of a terrorist cell in custody. They believe that the man they are holding knows of an impending attack that could kill thousands. The attack can be prevented only if the police find out its details, which the detainee knows. The suspect refuses to talk, however, and conventional interrogation techniques either will not break him down or would take too much time. Under those circumstances, would it be right to use physical force to give him the "third degree"?

Although this scenario is extreme, it makes the point that there are two sides to the debate over confessions. Critics of *Miranda* argue that the Supreme Court focused only on the suspect and ignored the rest of society, especially victims of crime. As Justice White wrote in his dissent in *Miranda*:

The real concern is not the unfortunate consequences of this new decision on the criminal law ... but the impact on those who rely on the public authority for protection and who, without it, can only engage in violent self-help with guns, knives and the help of their neighbors similarly inclined. There is, of course, a saving factor: the next victims are uncertain, unnamed and unrepresented in this case.[36]

Today's criminals are more dangerous than ever.

Today, we find ourselves facing criminals that the *Miranda* Court might never have imagined, including serial killers, organizations that smuggle weapons and drugs, human traffickers, and terrorists. The police are still obliged to abide by the now 40-year-old *Miranda* standard, however. After the Court handed down the *Escobedo* ruling, New York City Police Commissioner Michael J. Murphy observed, "What the Court is doing is akin to requiring one boxer to fight by Marquis of Queensbury rules while permitting the other to butt, gouge and bite."[37] Terrorists were not a high priority for New York's police commissioner during the 1960s, but they certainly are today, and they have demonstrated their unwillingness to "play by the rules." As the September 11, 2001, attacks demonstrated, terrorists are willing to commit acts of war and, at the same, flout the laws of armed conflict by disguising their status as fighters and targeting innocent civilians.

Terrorism is usually considered a strategy of warfare, but it has also been described as organized crime on a global scale. Many believe that we must rethink our approach toward fighting crime in light of the threat of terrorism. When the world learned that aggressive interrogation methods were used on suspected members of the al Qaeda terrorist organization, the American government defended those methods, arguing that soldiers were dealing with hardened fighters who would not respond to conventional techniques. Terrorists also pose a much greater threat than criminals such as Ernesto Miranda, and it is more important to stop

THE LETTER OF THE LAW

18 U.S.C. §3501, the Voluntary Confession Statute

Language in *Miranda* appeared to invite Congress and the states to explore alternatives to the rule laid down by the justices:

> Our decision in no way creates a constitutional straitjacket which will handicap sound efforts at reform, nor is it intended to have this effect. We encourage Congress and the States to continue their laudable search for increasingly effective ways of protecting the rights of the individual while promoting efficient enforcement of our criminal laws.[*]

Members of Congress, many of whom had reacted strongly to *Miranda*, took the Court up on its apparent offer. They added Title 18, §3501, to the United States Code.

Subsection (a) of that section provided that, in a federal criminal case, a confession "shall be admissible in evidence if it is voluntarily given." Subsection (b) required the judge, in determining the issue of voluntariness, to take into consideration "all the circumstances surrounding the giving of the confession," including the following:

(1) the time elapsing between arrest and arraignment of the defendant making the confession, if it was made after arrest and before arraignment,

(2) whether such defendant knew the nature of the offense with which he was charged or of which he was suspected at the time of making the confession,

(3) whether or not such defendant was advised or knew that he was not required to make any statement and that any such statement could be used against him,

(4) whether or not such defendant had been advised prior to questioning of his right to the assistance of counsel; and

(5) whether or not such defendant was without the assistance of counsel when questioned and when giving such confession.

Critics of §3501 argued that it was not an alternative to the *Miranda* rule but instead an attempt to overrule *Miranda* and reinstate the pre-*Miranda* voluntariness standard. In *Dickerson v. United States* (2000), the Court agreed that §3501 was an attempt to overrule *Miranda*. The *Dickerson* Court reaffirmed *Miranda* and, in doing so, ruled that §3501 could not be used in federal criminal cases.

[*]*Miranda v. Arizona*, 384 U.S. 436, 467 (1966).

them before they act than to punish them afterward. As Professor John Taylor observed:

> When the focus of investigation is not punishment but prevention—that is, when interrogation is designed not to obtain a confession but to elicit intelligence about terrorist activities—then the fundamental question becomes political rather than constitutional: how much and what sort of coercion are we willing to tolerate in order to gain information that may help prevent future terrorist attacks?[38]

In his *Miranda* dissent, Justice White argued that the majority's approach to interrogation would slow down police work in cases where time was of the essence and where national security was threatened. Pursuing terrorists qualifies under both criteria.

Finally, there is evidence that *Miranda* benefits the dangerous offenders more than poor or ignorant ones. Professor Paul Cassell believes that *Miranda* has led to thousands of "lost confessions." He observed:

> What might be called crimes of passion or emotion—murder, rape and assault—were apparently unaffected by *Miranda*, while crimes of deliberation—robbery, larceny, vehicle theft and possibly burglary—were affected. These categories are oversimplifications; obviously there are coolly calculated murders and impulsive car thefts. But if the generalizations are more often correct than incorrect, they correspond with the larger body of evidence suggesting that *Miranda* more substantially affects police success in dealing with repeat offenders and professional criminals.[39]

It is even possible that a suspected terrorist could go free on account of *Miranda*. In the criminal case that followed al Qaeda's bombings of American embassies in Kenya and Tanzania in 1998, U.S. District Judge Leonard Sand ruled in *United States v. Bin Laden* that the privilege against self-incrimination—and to the extent possible, the *Miranda* rule—protected defendants who were interrogated overseas. Judge Sand reasoned that the Fifth Amendment applies to any person who is put on trial in this country, even if he is a noncitizen and his alleged crimes occurred outside the United States. His ruling was not appealed, and it is unclear whether higher courts would reach the same conclusion.

The *Miranda* court ignored the interests of crime victims.

The timing of *Miranda* could not have been worse. As journalist Liva Baker noted,

> Each year the FBI published the ominous news in its *Uniform Crime Reports*: a 6 percent rise in serious crimes in 1962 over 1961, a 10 percent rise in 1963 over 1962, 13 percent in 1964 over 1963. Since 1958, the organization had reported in 1964, the incidence of crime had been growing six times faster than the American population.[40]

Professor Cassell believes that *Miranda* made an already-serious crime problem even worse. In his opinion, "No legacy of the Warren Court has been more devastating to the first civil right of individuals, the right to be protected from attack."[41] In his *Miranda* dissent, Justice White made a similar argument:

> More than the human dignity of the accused is involved; the human personality of others in the society must also be preserved. Thus the values reflected by the privilege are not the sole desideratum; society's interest in the general security is of equal weight. . . .
>
> The most basic function of any government is to provide for the security of the individual and of his property. These ends of society are served by the criminal laws which for the most part are aimed at the prevention of crime. Without the reasonably effective performance of the task of preventing private violence and retaliation, it is idle to talk about human dignity and civilized values.[42]

John Walker Lindh, seen above in an undated photo, was a young man from California who converted to Islam and fought with the Taliban in Afghanistan against the United States. Before he pleaded guilty to several crimes, his lawyers argued in court that his confession had been coerced.

Opponents of *Miranda* are especially critical of its use of the exclusionary rule to deal with violations. Unless the police prove that they obtained a suspect's statement in compliance with the *Miranda* rule, the judge will exclude that statement—

even if the police acted in good faith and the defendant confessed of his own free will. Gary Nelson, the assistant attorney
general who represented Arizona in Ernesto Miranda's appeal,
said of the *Miranda* rule, "Unless you cross all the t's and dot all
the i's you are out of luck."[43] Critics insist that the exclusionary

Miranda on the Battlefield? *United States v. Lindh*

During the invasion of Afghanistan, Americans were surprised to learn that one
of their fellow citizens had fought alongside the enemy. They were even more
surprised when he accused his government of having denied him his rights as a
citizen—including his *Miranda* rights.

The American's name was John Walker Lindh. He was a young man from California who converted to a fundamentalist form of Islam and traveled to Afghanistan.
After Lindh was captured there by coalition forces, he was questioned by military
interrogators and, later, by FBI agents. He admitted to the agents that he had
fought alongside the Taliban. The Justice Department charged him with a number
of crimes, including conspiring to kill Americans overseas and providing support
to foreign terrorist organizations. Those crimes are punishable by life in prison.
The attorney general also left open the possibility of treason charges, which carry
the death penalty.

At first, *United States v. Lindh* seemed to be an open-and-shut case. The evidence
against Lindh was his confession, which, according to the government, he had
given freely to the FBI after being read his *Miranda* rights. Lindh also acknowledged that he understood his rights and decided to waive them.

Later, however, a different version of what happened in Afghanistan emerged.
As Professor John Taylor explained:

> He was bound naked to a stretcher, kept cold and hungry in a windowless
> shipping container, and denied medical care for a bullet wound. The FBI
> agent informed him of his rights but made clear that no lawyers were avail-
> able in Afghanistan, a point he repeated when Lindh asked to consult one.
> He did not inform Lindh that his father had retained an attorney who was
> trying to see him, or pass along his father's message....
>
>   Under these circumstances, Lindh waived his rights and made incrimi-
> nating statements, apparently to avoid being returned to the conditions of
> physical privation in which he had been kept.*

rule was not intended by the Framers. They point out that no equivalent rule exists in English common law, which suggests that it was invented by well-meaning judges and not derived from the Constitution. In addition, they insist that judges' decisions to bar confessions do not punish the police officers

The defense moved to suppress Lindh's statement. It argued that the FBI agents violated the *Miranda* rule by questioning him after he had asked to see a lawyer, that his waiver of rights was not intelligent and voluntary, and that his incriminating statement had been coerced. The government countered that Lindh did not ask for a lawyer until after he had confessed and that he had spoken freely to military personnel and FBI agents. It also argued that Lindh was not entitled to *Miranda* warnings because American soldiers who debriefed captured enemy combatants did not have to follow *Miranda*.

The issue of why a person was interrogated does not arise in an American police station, but it does in a war zone. The soldiers who questioned Lindh were interested in gathering intelligence about the Taliban, not in building a criminal case. In fact, military interrogators were instructed to read a prisoner his or her rights if the questions being asked were likely to produce evidence of criminal conduct.

Because Lindh's statement was at the heart of the case against him, the ruling on the motion to suppress would likely determine guilt or innocence. On July 15, 2002, however, the *Miranda* issue became moot—that is, it no longer had a bearing on Lindh's fate—when the two sides agreed to a plea bargain. Lindh pleaded guilty to reduced charges that carried a 20-year prison sentence and agreed not to talk to the media about the case. He avoided a harsher sentence, and the government avoided the bad publicity that might have resulted from the case.

The issue of whether the courts view a confession taken on a battlefield differently from one taken in a police station went unresolved. Another issue that relates to terrorism remains unresolved as well: whether *Miranda* protects a *noncitizen* who is questioned overseas and whose statement is later used in a criminal case here. Legal experts believe that both issues will eventually come before the Supreme Court.

*John B. Taylor, *The Right to Counsel and the Privilege Against Self-Incrimination.* Santa Barbara, CA: ABC-CLIO, Inc., 2004, p. 271.

who violate the *Miranda* rule but members of the public who are put at added risk of becoming crime victims. In Ernesto Miranda's case, a conviction for a serious crime was overturned because the police had violated a rule that had not yet come into existence.

Confessions remain an important crime-fighting tool.

In Cold Blood, a book by Truman Capote, detailed the murders of four members of a Kansas family. After *Miranda* was decided, Capote told a Senate committee that, if *Miranda* had been the law at the time of the murders, defendants Richard Hickock and Perry Smith would have gone "scot-free." Hickock's and Smith's confessions were a key piece of evidence at their trial. Over the years, many serious crimes have been solved as the result of the offender confessing his guilt. Obtaining confessions was considered good police work and beneficial to society. As Justice White wrote in his *Miranda* dissent, "Particularly when corroborated, as where the police have confirmed the accused's disclosure of the hiding place of implements or fruits of the crime, such confessions have the highest reliability and significantly contribute to the certitude with which we may believe the accused is guilty."[44] Fellow dissenter John Harlan made a related observation, "Society has always paid a stiff price for law and order, and peaceful interrogation is not one of the dark moments of the law."[45]

Conservative legal scholar Bruce Fein offered an example of how the *Miranda* rule could undermine an otherwise sound investigation:

> The police arrest a murder suspect and return to headquarters for a videotaped interrogation. Refreshments are provided, and a police inspector with the shrewdness of Sherlock Holmes elicits a confession by playing on the suspect's emotional vulnerabilities. Attempts to gather incriminating evidence through search warrants and witnesses prove futile.

At trial, the videotape is authenticated and categorically dis-credits any claim of police coercion. The confession would be excluded under *Miranda* and the prosecution foiled, however, because the suspect was not previously informed of his right not to cooperate and to the presence and assistance of a lawyer.[46]

Fein's example is extreme—and is intended to be. Still, it illustrates what can happen when following procedure is given a higher priority than searching for the truth.

The public demands stronger measures against violent crime.

Richard Nixon, the Republican candidate for president in 1968, ran on a "law and order" platform and attacked the Warren Court. He told voters, "I think that some of the decisions of the Supreme Court have weakened the peace forces as against the criminal forces in this country. I support legislation to restore the balance."[7] Most Americans agreed. Nixon and Alabama governor George Wallace, who attacked the Court even more forcefully than Nixon, won a combined 57 percent of the 1968 presidential vote. The result suggests that Americans wanted "strict constructionists" on the bench.

Americans remain highly sympathetic toward victims' rights, so much so that tough new criminal laws often bear the names of the victims. They still believe that criminals pay too low a price for their actions and that the courts are part of the problem. Lawyer and author Wendy Kaminer interviewed a prosecuting attorney who commented on the public anger at the justice system. The prosecutor described a movie in which a police officer battered the "bad guy" while reading him his *Miranda* rights and then told Kaminer, "The people in the movie theater are standing up and cheering because they know that our side is losing, and the very notion that criminals need to be advised of their constitutional rights—the only place it'll ever wash is in this country.[48]

Popular television dramas such as "CSI," "Law & Order," and "Without a Trace" favorably portray the police and prosecutors. Those programs might reflect Americans' belief that they are under siege by criminals and that the authorities are allies, not adversaries. What is behind that belief? Kaminer explained:

> The politics of crime control sometimes seems a simple matter of arithmetic. There are more crime victims than criminal

Ernesto Miranda: The Rest of the Story

After the Supreme Court ruled in his favor, Ernesto Miranda remained in prison to serve his sentence for the robbery conviction that his lawyers had not appealed to the Court. He was paroled in December 1972. After his release, Miranda sometimes could be found on the courthouse steps in Phoenix, selling autographed cards with the now-famous *Miranda* warnings. After several incidents that involved drugs, Miranda's parole was revoked and he went back to prison.

Miranda was released again in December 1975, and returned to life on the lower rungs of society. That environment soon proved deadly. On January 31, 1976, he was stabbed to death in a fight over two dollars in a barroom card game. The police believed that two part-time field hands, Fernando Rodríguez and Esezquiel Moreno, had killed him. Author Gary Stuart described what happened next:

> The investigation of Miranda's murder had obviously been conducted in full compliance with *Miranda* warnings. Both suspects had voluntarily waived their rights and told police their stories without benefit of counsel's presence. However, unlike the 1963 police investigation of Miranda himself, no confessions were extracted and no one went to jail for the crime. Fernando Rodriguez and Eseziquel Moreno, released pending further investigation, both disappeared and were never seen again.*

Several months later, the police closed the file on Ernesto Miranda's murder. No one was ever punished for it.

*Gary L. Stuart, *Miranda: The Story of America's Right to Remain Silent*. Tucson: University of Arizona Press, 2004, p. 99.

defendants, particularly among the voting public, so there are likely to be more conservatives than liberals on the subject of crime—many more. Given the daily barrage of crime reports on TV news and in daily papers and the low clearance rates for violent crimes, it's likely that even people who've never been victims or defendants worry more about being victimized by violence than being prosecuted for it.[49]

There is a final irony to the *Miranda* debate: Although that decision was intended to make the justice system fairer to the accused, it might have done them more harm than good over the long run. *Miranda* helped create a backlash that elected a president who appointed more conservative justices to the Supreme Court. Those appointees not only limited the scope of the *Miranda* rule, but also cut back on other constitutional protections enjoyed by criminal defendants.

Summary

The *Miranda* decision focused entirely on the rights of suspects and ignored the interests of the rest of society, especially citizens put at added risk of becoming crime victims. The *Miranda* Court disregarded the wishes of Americans, who wanted the authorities to act more aggressively to curb a worsening crime problem. The balance struck by *Miranda* has become even more unjustifiable because today's criminals are more dangerous than those of Ernesto Miranda's era. Confessions remain essential to convicting and punishing these criminals, and the police should be applauded for their efforts to obtain them—not bound by technical rules.

The *Miranda* Rule Encourages Civilized Police Behavior

E rnesto Miranda signed a statement that acknowledged that he understood his rights and thus that his confession was voluntary. He gave a different version of his interrogation when his case was on appeal, however:

> Once they get you in a little room and they start badgering you one way or the other, "you better tell us . . . or we're going to throw the book at you" . . . that is what was told to me. They would throw the book at me. They would try to give me all the time they could. They thought there was even the possibility that there was something wrong with me. They would try to help me, get me medical care if I needed it. . . . And I haven't had any sleep since the day before. I'm tired. I just got off work, and they have me and they are interrogating me. They mention first one crime, then another one, they are certain I

am the person . . . knowing what a penitentiary is like, a person has to be frightened, scared. And not knowing if he'll be able to get back up and go home.[50]

In overturning Miranda's rape conviction, the Supreme Court described the police station as an "inherently coercive" setting. More than 40 years later, that is still the case.

Abusing suspects is contrary to basic American values.

In 2004, people around the world were shocked by graphic photos that depicted the mistreatment of Iraqi prisoners by American troops at the Abu Ghraib prison in Baghdad. Some of the abuses occurred while soldiers were interrogating the prisoners about their involvement in attacks against Americans and possible links to terrorist organizations. What happened at those facilities? According to Professor John Taylor:

> By early 2003 it had been reported that the rules of the game appeared to allow all methods short of outright torture to disorient prisoners and break their will. Techniques of physical and psychological pressure include subjection to uncomfortable positions, nudity, constant light or darkness, temperature extremes, sleep deprivation, and irregular meals and medical attention, in some cases over a period of months.[51]

Human-rights groups, as well as millions of Americans, were shocked by what they saw and read. They considered the abuse of prisoners a human-rights violation. Some, such as author Gary Stuart, worried that such violations could harm this country in the long run. He wrote:

> We would do well to remember, however, that if, in the effort to solve the problems *Miranda* has posed to law

enforcement, we return to the days when law enforcement was silent on the rights of suspects—be they home-grown thieves or foreign-trained terrorists—then those people seeking to destroy democracy itself . . . will have obtained one of their objectives.[52]

Whether it happens in prisons overseas or police stations at home, the abuse of people in custody offends basic American standards of human rights and common decency.

"Freeborn" John Lilburn and the Privilege Against Self-Incrimination

Many in the legal community believe that the origins of the *Miranda* rule extend back many centuries into English common law, which recognized the privilege of a criminal defendant not to incriminate himself—that is, accuse himself of a crime. That privilege was the basis of the Fifth Amendment to our Constitution.

In medieval times, two different models of criminal justice developed. On the European continent, an "inquisitorial" system took hold. The accused was brought before a judge and directed to answer questions, often under conditions of torture. Under the inquisitorial system, accused persons were required to take an oath *ex officio* that bound them to tell the truth. The proceedings were stacked against the accused. They did not know their accusers, what the charge was, or what the evidence against them was. If accused persons refused to take the oath, they risked being tortured until they changed their minds. If they did take it, they risked either incriminating themselves or being punished for perjury—that is, making false statements under oath.

English courts, on the other hand, developed an "accusatorial" system of justice in which the Crown had to prove the defendant's guilt. Lawyers rather than judges questioned the accused, and a jury determined guilt or innocence. This system did not develop overnight: It took many centuries for English courts to develop the procedures that we take for granted in a modern criminal trial.

Another factor complicated English law: For centuries, two separate court systems existed side by side, one established by the Church and the other by the

Coercive interrogation violates human dignity.

Today's police use tactics that might have astonished the justices who sat on the *Miranda* Court. The Phoenix detectives who obtained Ernesto Miranda's confession resorted to simple deception. Today's interrogators use much more sophisticated techniques aimed at breaking the suspect's will and pressuring him or her to make incriminating statements.

The police are aware of the human desire to seek forgiveness. In his book about the *Miranda* case, Gary Stuart reflected:

Crown. Church courts made use of inquisitorial procedures; the royal courts did not. That distinction broke down when England suffered political and religious conflicts during the sixteenth and seventeenth centuries. Special courts were created to deal with suspected enemies of the state. The most notorious such court was the Court of Star Chamber.

One of the best-known defendants brought before the Court of Star Chamber was "Freeborn" John Lilburne, an opponent of England's established church. In 1637, Lilburne was charged with heresy. When he refused to enter a plea, the judges ordered him whipped, put on public display in a pillory, and thrown in prison. Professor Richard Leo explained the significance of his case:

> Lilburne's refusal to answer questions before the Court of Star Chamber subsequently came to represent the idea that no man should be compelled to testify against himself, a right that citizens commonly began to assert in criminal trials. By the end of the seventeenth century, the privilege against compelled testimony had become a well-established common law right.[*]

In his majority opinion in *Miranda*, Chief Justice Warren paid homage to Lilburne, suggesting that his trial was a critical event leading to the Fifth Amendment as we know it.

[*]Richard A. Leo, "The Impact of *Miranda* Revisited." J. Crim. L. & Criminology 86(3): 621, 629 (Spring 1996).

Whether innate or acquired early in life, the desire to confess—to take responsibility for a perceived misdeed—is no
doubt a deep-seated impulse in us all. . . .

There is, however, a curious aspect to our impulse to confess. We feel that in the act of contrition resides an implicit
covenant: If I confess, I will be forgiven by the authority with
which I have formed this covenant, for in the confession itself
I make restitution.

For the higher authority, however, the admission of
wrongdoing is not the end. The ancient god of retribution
must be served; the wrongdoer must pay for what he did, with
his wealth, his liberty, or his life.[53]

Although the third degree has largely disappeared from
American police stations, some believe that today's police
practice psychological coercion that is, in some respects, just
as demeaning. This argument is not new. In *Miranda*, the
Court observed, "It is obvious that such an interrogation environment is created for no purpose other than to subjugate the
individual to the will of his examiner. This atmosphere carries
its own badge of intimidation. To be sure, this is not physical
intimidation, but it is equally destructive of human dignity."[54]
Some believe that, after the September 11 terrorist attacks,
we have paid too little attention to the human rights of those
in custody.

Police misconduct breeds disrespect for the law.

When the Constitution was written, magistrates—lower-rank-
ing members of the judiciary—questioned suspects before
trial. By the nineteenth century, the role of magistrates diminished and the police assumed the responsibility of obtaining
statements that would be used in court. Author John Taylor
observed, "Because obtaining a confession is often the sim-
plest way to solve a case, police have a continuing incentive to

employ methods that will achieve that result."[55] In *Escobedo v. Illinois*, the Court quoted Dean Wigmore, a leading authority on the law of evidence. Wigmore warned of the consequences of unchecked police interrogation:

> The simple and peaceful process of questioning breeds a readiness to resort to bullying and to physical force and torture. If there is a right to an answer, there soon seems to be a right to the expected answer—that is, to a confession of guilt. Thus the legitimate use grows into the unjust abuse; ultimately, the innocent are jeopardized by the encroachments of a bad system. Such seems to have been the course of experience in those legal systems where the privilege was not recognized.[56]

Deception—much of which is tolerated by the courts—has replaced brute force as a means of extracting confessions. Critics point out that, although we expect our public officials to be honest, some police officers resort to unethical and dishonest tactics in obtaining incriminating statements. They also point out that, if officers lie inside the interrogation room, what would stop them from lying to their superiors or even lying in court? In 1952, FBI Director J. Edgar Hoover wrote of the importance of law-enforcement officers abiding by the law:

> Law enforcement, however, in defeating the criminal, must maintain inviolate the historic liberties of the individual. To turn back the criminal, yet, by so doing, destroy the dignity of the individual, would be a hollow victory. . . .
>
> We can have the Constitution, the best laws in the land, and the most honest reviews by courts—but unless the law enforcement profession is steeped in the democratic tradition, maintains the highest in ethics, and makes its work a career of honor, civil liberties will continually—and without end—be violated.[57]

It has also been argued that dishonest police work ultimately diminishes the department's effectiveness in fighting crime. Professor Richard Leo and coauthor Jerome Skolnick, a professor at the John Jay College of Criminal Justice, explained:

Suing Over *Miranda* Violations: *Chavez v. Martinez*

What recourse does a suspect have when the police obtain his confession in violation of *Miranda* but never use it against him in a criminal case? In *Chavez v. Martinez,* 538 U.S. 760 (2005), that issue came before the Supreme Court.

This case began when two Oxnard, California, police officers got into an altercation with Olivero Martinez. One of the officers shot Martinez, seriously wounding him. Martinez was taken to the hospital, where he was in great pain and thought he was going to die. While Martinez was being treated, Ben Chavez, a patrol supervisor, questioned him about the altercation. Chavez never read Martinez his *Miranda* rights. Thinking that he would be denied medical treatment unless he told what happened, Martinez admitted that he took a gun from one of the officers and that he was a regular heroin user.

Martinez was never charged with a crime, and his incriminating statements were never used against him. Nevertheless, he filed a civil lawsuit against Chavez and the city under the Civil Rights Act of 1871 (Title 42, §1983 of the United States Code). In order to succeed in a §1983 case, a person must prove that a constitutional right had been violated. Martinez argued that Chavez had violated the Fifth Amendment by not following *Miranda* and by coercing him into making incriminating statements. The lower federal courts ruled in Martinez's favor, and Chavez appealed to the Supreme Court.

A majority of the Court ruled that Chavez had not violated Martinez's Fifth Amendment rights. Speaking for four justices, Justice Clarence Thomas concluded that the only remedy for a Fifth Amendment violation was exclusion of the defendant's statement at trial. In his view, coercion by the police, by itself, was not a violation because the Fifth Amendment applied to criminal "cases" and police questioning did not constitute a "case." He added that Martinez never was a "witness" against himself and never had been placed under oath. Justice Thomas also pointed out that a violation of the *Miranda* rule was not necessarily a violation of the Fifth Amendment itself.

Police lying might not have mattered so much to police work in other times and places in American history. But today, when urban juries are increasingly composed of jurors disposed to be distrustful of police, deception by police during

Justices David Souter and Stephen Breyer agreed that Martinez had no Fifth Amendment claim. They left open the possibility that civil lawsuits might be necessary to protect citizens' Fifth Amendment rights, but Martinez had not convinced them that he should be allowed to sue. They also expressed concern that if the Court ruled in Martinez's favor, every involuntary confession could result in a lawsuit.

Three justices dissented. Justice Anthony Kennedy argued that the Fifth Amendment applied "at the time and place police use compulsion to extract a statement from a suspect," even if that statement is never introduced at trial. He warned that the majority's narrow reading of the Fifth Amendment sent the wrong message: "To tell our whole legal system that when conducting a criminal investigation police officials can use severe compulsion or even torture with no present violation of the right against compelled self-incrimination can only diminish a celebrated provision in the Bill of Rights."

Justice John Paul Stevens described Chavez's actions as "the functional equivalent of an attempt to obtain an involuntary confession from a prisoner by torturous methods" and noted that earlier Court decisions had found that "unusually coercive" interrogation procedures were unconstitutional. Justice Ruth Bader Ginsberg agreed that a violation occurred when the police used "severe compulsion" to extract a statement and added that the Fifth Amendment laid down a standard of civilized behavior.

The majority's rejection of Martinez's Fifth Amendment claim was not the end of the case. Seven justices voted to send the case back to the lower courts to determine whether Chavez's actions denied Martinez due process of law. Two justices dissented. Justice Thomas maintained that Martinez had no due process claim because Chavez's actions were not "outrageous" or "shocking to the conscience." Justice Antonin Scalia agreed and added that, because Martinez had not raised a due process claim in the lower courts, it was too late for him to do so now.

interrogation offers yet another reason for disbelieving law enforcement witnesses when they take the stand, thus reducing police effectiveness as controllers of crime.[58]

Many observers of O.J. Simpson's criminal trial believe that the jury's not-guilty verdict was motivated in part by distrust of the Los Angeles police.

Miranda has encouraged the police to conduct more thorough investigations.

Confessions can become an attractive shortcut for painstaking—but more effective—police work. As Justice Ruth Bader Ginsberg recently remarked, "It is far pleasanter to sit comfortably in the shade rubbing red pepper into a poor devil's eyes than to go about in the sun hunting up evidence."[59] The *Miranda* Court noted that Ernesto Miranda's appeal, and the three appeals decided together with it, "present graphic examples of the over-statement of the 'need' for confessions. In each case, authorities conducted investigations ranging up to five days in duration despite the presence, through standard investigating practices, of considerable evidence against each defendant."[60]

For the most part, the consequences that *Miranda*'s critics feared failed to materialize. After some problems immediately after the decision, the nation's police departments adapted. In fact, supporters believe that *Miranda* has improved the quality of police work. According to author Liva Baker,

> *Miranda* had contributed something to the professionalization of the patrolman who could no longer rely on the quick and easy confession but now had to dig for evidence in his crime solving, a development to which the increased workloads of the crime laboratories testified.[61]

Professor Richard Leo has pointed out four positive effects of *Miranda*. First, it had a civilizing influence on police interrogation behavior and has professionalized police practices. Second, it transformed the culture and discourse of detective work. Third, it increased the public's awareness of constitutional rights. Finally, it led the police to develop more specialized, more sophisticated, and seemingly more effective interrogation techniques.

The *Miranda* Court pointed out that the FBI had compiled "an exemplary record" of effective law enforcement despite having a policy of warning a person, before questioning, of his right to remain silent and to consult with an attorney, and that, since 1952, it had been Bureau policy to give suspects *Miranda*-like warnings. In fact, long-time FBI Director J. Edgar Hoover

The Retrials of Ernesto Miranda and Charles Dickerson

Critics often argue that the *Miranda* rule has made it too easy for criminals to go free on technicalities. They might be surprised to learn what actually happened to the defendants who won in the celebrated decisions of *Miranda v. Arizona* and *Dickerson v. United States*.

Ernesto Miranda was tried a second time for sexually assaulting Jane Smith. This time, the prosecution was barred from using the statement that he had given the police while he was interrogated. It appeared as though Miranda would go free until Twila Hoffman, his former common-law wife, informed the police that he had told her about the crime. After what was described as a "nine-day constitutional chess match" among the lawyers, the judge ruled that Miranda's "confession" to Hoffman was far enough removed from his interrogation by the police that it could be admitted as evidence. That was enough to convict Miranda. Arizona's highest court affirmed the conviction, and Miranda's lawyers asked the Supreme Court to review the case. This time, the justices refused.

Charles Dickerson fared no better than Miranda. After his victory in the Supreme Court, the government tried him a second time for bank robbery and other crimes. At the retrial, the actual robber, Jimmy Rochester, testified that Dickerson drove the getaway car. Dickerson's lawyers decided to put him on the stand to tell his version of the story. Once he testified, however, he opened the door to impeachment evidence—which included the statement that the police had obtained in violation of the *Miranda* rule. The jury found him guilty, and the United States Court of Appeals for the Fourth Circuit affirmed his conviction.

Ernesto Miranda (above) listens to court proceedings during the 1967 retrial of his case. Although his first conviction was overturned by the U.S. Supreme Court, he was convicted a second time based on new testimony, and the Supreme Court refused to review this decision.

insisted that good police work and fair play did not conflict. He wrote, "Law enforcement, however, in defeating the criminal, must maintain inviolate the historic liberties of the individual.

To turn back the criminal, yet, by so doing, destroy the dignity of the individual, would be a hollow victory."[62]

Summary

Although the third degree has largely disappeared from interrogation rooms, police use psychological tactics that are equally coercive. As the Court observed in *Miranda*, those tactics are destructive of human dignity. Coercive tactics are unnecessary because the police routinely collect evidence using other means. In fact, *Miranda* has encouraged the police to resort to alternatives to confessions. Coercion is also counterproductive because it breeds disrespect for the law and distrust of the police, thus making it harder to enforce the law.

Miranda Has Hindered the Fight Against Crime

I n 1983, Ronnie Dale Gaspard lured a young woman named Denise Sanders to a Texas lake and shot her in the head. He killed Sanders because she had testified against members of Gaspard's motorcycle gang, the Bandidos, and her testimony sent some of them to jail on drug trafficking charges. Journalist Alexander Nguyen explained what happened next:

> [The police] seized Gaspard and charged him with the murder. And then something happened that is the stuff of bad television drama. The police read Gaspard his *Miranda* rights. Gaspard asked for a lawyer but then confessed before the lawyer arrived. A judge later threw out Gaspard's confession because it had been taken in violation of the *Miranda* rule. Gaspard walked out free, smirking. "Nothing ever bothered me as much as seeing that guy walk out of the courthouse,"

the assistant district attorney was quoted as saying. "But there's nothing I can do. He is off and free."[63]

Although Gaspard's story is shocking, critics of *Miranda* insist that it is not an isolated case. They believe that thousands of violent crimes have gone unpunished because of the obstacles that *Miranda* put in the way of the police.

Miranda has cost the police thousands of confessions.

Before he was named a federal judge in 2002, Professor Paul Cassell sought to prove that *Miranda* had a devastating impact on the police's ability to solve crimes. At the heart of the problem were "lost confessions"—confessions that the police would have been able to obtain before *Miranda* but no longer could. Cassell first presented his "lost confessions" study in an article[64] in a law review in 1996; since then, he has published numerous articles that attack *Miranda*.

One method Cassell used to estimate *Miranda*'s impact was to compare statistics compiled by police departments before *Miranda* with those compiled afterward. Cassell summarized what he found:

> One leading study, done in Philadelphia, reported that, before *Miranda*, an estimated 45 per cent of all criminal suspects made confessions to police officers; following *Miranda*, that figure dropped to approximately 20 per cent. Another study, done in New York City, found that confession rates fell from 49 per cent to 15 per cent. In Pittsburgh, the confession rate among suspected robbers and murderers fell from 60 per cent to 30 per cent. Adverse effects on confessions were also reported in Chicago, Kansas City, Brooklyn, and New Orleans.[65]

Using those and other studies, Cassell calculated the percentage of "lost confessions." The reliable data from the before-and-after studies show that confession rates fell by about 16 percentage points after *Miranda*. In other words, if the confession rate was 60 percent before *Miranda*, it was 44 percent after—meaning that, in about one of every six criminal cases, *Miranda* resulted in a lost confession. Reliable studies also indicate that confessions are needed to obtain a conviction in about 24 percent of all cases. Combining these two figures produces the result that about 3.8 percent (16 percent multiplied by 24 percent) of criminal cases in this country are lost because of the restrictions imposed by *Miranda*.[66]

The studies that Professor Cassell used were decades old, but he found more recent studies from a number of cities that suggested that confession rates are still lower than they were during the pre-*Miranda* era.

Because of *Miranda*, thousands of crimes have gone unsolved.

There are no national studies that compare pre- and post-*Miranda* confession rates. Professor Cassell instead used clearance rates, for which national figures do exist. The clearance rate is the percentage of known crimes that the police are able to solve. For example, when Ernesto Miranda made his now-famous confession, he admitted not only to raping Jane Smith but also to abducting and robbing two other women who had also complained to the police. Miranda's confession thus enabled the police to "clear" a number of crimes.

Based on his analysis of studies such as those quoted above, Cassell estimated that the clearance rate fell by approximately 16 percent after the Court decided *Miranda*. He and University of Utah economics Professor Richard Fowles found that clearance rates fell nationwide immediately after *Miranda* and remained at those lower levels for the next 30 years. Cassell and Fowles calculated that *Miranda* led to a 6.7-percent decline in clearance rates for violent crimes and a 2.2-percent decline for property crimes. Those percentages translated into 28,000 fewer convictions per year for violent crimes and 79,000

Chief Justice Earl Warren poses for a formal portrait in his judicial robes in December 1953. Warren wrote the controversial majority opinion in *Miranda*, which, though unpopular, would go on to be integrated into the public's perception of criminal law.

fewer convictions for property crimes. They also estimated that 500,000 convictions for other crimes per year are lost on account of *Miranda*. Professor Cassell called those estimates "quite conservative" and observed that "They capture only *Miranda*'s impact on crime clearances, ignoring some of the effects on prosecutions and convictions at later points in the criminal justice system."[67] Cassell and others argue that *Miranda*'s costs to society do not end with lost convictions: The other costs include unrecovered stolen property and contraband, criminal careers that are allowed to continue, and time spent by police and prosecutors on pretrial motions on the admissibility of confessions rather than proving defendants' guilt. Bruce Fein also observed that:

> Searching for incriminating evidence despite voluntary and reliable confessions is not without cost. FBI statistics show that only one in five felonies leads to an arrest; in four of

Earl Warren and the "Warren Court"

Chief Justice Earl Warren, who wrote the majority opinion in *Miranda*, was one of the most unpopular figures in American public life at the time of that case. His career on the Court surprised most Americans, including President Dwight D. Eisenhower, who nominated him to the Court in 1953.

Warren was a Republican whose first elected office was that of district attorney in the San Francisco Bay area. He later served as attorney general of California and became popular for taking a hard line toward the left wing and organized labor—and especially for favoring the internment of Japanese Americans after the Japanese attack on Pearl Harbor. Warren was so popular that he was elected governor and held that office for 10 years. As the governor of a large state, Warren became a force in national politics. He was the Republican Party's nominee for vice president in 1948 and, four years later, helped Eisenhower win the presidential nomination.

Warren was an unusual choice for the Court. His entire career in public life had been at the state level, and he had never served as a judge before. As journalist Liva Baker noted, "There was little about his official conduct during those 19 years in the front lines of local law enforcement to suggest the scrupulousness with which later in his life he would defend the constitutional rights of the criminally accused."* In naming Warren to the Court, President Eisenhower said, "I certainly wanted a man whose reputation for integrity, honesty, middle-of-the-road philosophy, experience in Government, experience in the law, were all such as to convince the United States that here was a man who had no ends except to serve the United States, and nothing else."**

five incidents, no one is apprehended. Insofar as *Miranda* compels investigators to prove guilt without confessions, law enforcement is diverted from solving other serious crimes.[68]

In light of these findings, why has *Miranda* remained on the law books? Cassell has maintained that

the impact of *Miranda*, while extraordinarily detrimental to the criminal-justice system, is largely a hidden one, while the costs of such innovations as the exclusionary rule and habeas

During the 1960s, the Warren Court—the five-member majority headed by the chief justice—became a campaign issue. Presidential candidate Richard Nixon told an audience, "I think that some of the decisions of the Supreme Court have weakened the peace forces as against the criminal forces in this country," and added, "We need more strict constructionists on the highest court of the United States."***

Earl Warren's career as chief justice ended with his retirement in 1969. His replacement was Warren Burger, an appeals court judge who had once written about *Miranda*, "We are well on our way to forbidding *any* utterance of an accused to be used against him unless it is made in open court. Guilt or innocence becomes irrelevant in the criminal trial as we founder in a morass of artificial rules poorly conceived and often impossible of application."[†]

As President Nixon promised, the Burger Court halted the expansion of the rights of criminal suspects, including their *Miranda* rights. Ironically, however, the Burger Court is best known for handing down a decision as controversial as *Miranda*: the case of *Roe v. Wade*, 410 U.S. 133 (1973), which held that most states' restrictions on abortion were unconstitutional. Opponents of *Roe* accused the Court of creating constitutional rights—the same charge that was leveled at the five justices who voted in favor of *Miranda*.

*Liva Baker, *Miranda: Crime, Law, and Politics*. New York: Atheneum, 1983, p. 116.
**Ibid., p. 124
***Ibid. p. 246
†*Frazier v. United States*, 419 F.2d 1161, 1176 (D.C. Cir. 1969) (Burger, J., dissenting in part).

corpus are highly visible, in the form of kilos of cocaine being removed from the courtroom and repetitive criminal appeals inundating the justice system.[69]

According to his calculations, *Miranda* is responsible for even more lost convictions than the exclusionary rule in search-and-seizure cases, which is frequently attacked by law-enforcement advocates.

Miranda has not protected the innocent.

Professor Cassell found that *Miranda* has not only caused substantial harm to society but has also provided little protection to the innocent—which was a major goal of *Miranda*'s supporters. He explained, "The innocent are also jeopardized when police fail to obtain a truthful confession from the true perpetrator of a crime. That truthful confession could prevent suspicion from wrongfully falling on an innocent person and could even exonerate an innocent person who has been wrongfully charged with, or convicted of, a crime."[70] He went on to provide an example: "If the police apprehend an armed robber at the scene of the crime, he may invoke his *Miranda* rights and prevent police from learning that he has committed five other similar robberies. If an innocent person has been charged, or even convicted, for one of these other robberies, *Miranda* may well prevent his exoneration."[71]

In support of his argument, Cassell cited research into wrongful convictions done by Professor Samuel Gross of the University of Michigan. Professor Gross explained that, before *Miranda*, the typical way in which a miscarriage of justice was discovered was that the actual criminal was arrested on an unrelated charge and, after being held in custody for a day or two, confessed to all of the crimes charged to the misidentified suspect. He found that 54 percent of wrongful convictions that resulted from misidentification by eyewitnesses were uncovered when the actual criminal confessed.

Miranda was a failed experiment.

Justice John Harlan, a dissenter in *Miranda*, called the majority's approach to confessions "a hazardous experimentation." Forty years later, it is clear that the decision has had unintended—and detrimental—consequences to society.

When *Miranda* was argued before the Court, the National District Attorneys Association told the justices that warning suspects of their right to remain silent, without more, "will benefit only the recidivist [repeat offender] and the professional."[72] Professor Cassell's studies have borne that out: Professional criminals and repeat offenders are more likely to benefit from *Miranda* than are common criminals such as Ernesto Miranda. Even *Miranda*'s supporters concede that it has not "leveled the playing field."

Miranda has slowed down the justice system with pretrial motions and other proceedings. Although rules of evidence and procedure are essential to a fair trial, they can become self-defeating. During his confirmation hearing for the position of chief justice, Warren Burger told senators, "Procedure is what protects people. But procedure can carry so much armament that like King Philip's Spanish Armada on the way to England, the weight made the ships nonmanueverable and the British were able to sink those that did not sink by their own weight."[73] Procedural rulings also resulted in offenders such as Ronnie Dale Gaspard going free; cases such as his fuel the public perception that criminals are routinely set free because of technicalities.

In any event, critics argue that the *Miranda* rule has proven no more workable than the pre-*Miranda* "voluntariness" standard. In his dissent, Justice White warned:

> Today's decision leaves open such questions as whether the accused was in custody, whether his statements were spontaneous or the product of interrogation, whether the accused has effectively waived his rights, and whether nontestimonial evidence introduced at trial is the fruit of statements made during a prohibited interrogation, all of which are certain

to prove productive of uncertainty during investigation and litigation during prosecution.[74]

White was correct. As Justice Scalia wrote in his dissent in *Dickerson*:

Making *Miranda* Less Rigid: *Harris v. New York*

The Burger Court's first major decision that involved the *Miranda* rule was *Harris v. New York*, 401 U.S. 222 (1971). The case began when Viven Harris allegedly sold heroin to an undercover police officer in New Rochelle, New York, on two occasions. The police questioned Harris about the sales without first warning him that a lawyer would be appointed to him if he could not afford one.

At his trial on delivery-of-heroin charges, Harris took the stand in his own defense. He denied the first sale and claimed that the second sale was one of baking soda, not heroin. On cross-examination, the prosecutor asked Harris about statements he made to the police that were inconsistent with what he told the jury. The judge told the jurors that they could consider those statements only to determine whether he was believable, not whether he had sold heroin. The jury found Harris guilty of one of the two sales. New York's appellate courts upheld the conviction, and Harris appealed to the United States Supreme Court.

By a 5-to-4 vote, the Court upheld Harris's conviction. Chief Justice Warren Burger wrote the majority opinion. He concluded that, even though a confession taken in violation of *Miranda* could not be used directly to prove the defendant's guilt, it could be used to impeach his or her testimony. The chief justice stated, "It does not follow from *Miranda* that evidence inadmissible against an accused in the prosecution's case in chief is barred for all purposes." He pointed out that Viven Harris made the choice to take the stand and, once he did, he took the risk of being asked whether he was telling the truth. The chief justice found Harris's trial analogous to that in *Walder v. United States* (1954), in which the Court held that it was proper for the prosecution to use physical evidence obtained in an earlier unlawful search to impeach the defendant's testimony that he never possessed illegal drugs.

The chief justice also questioned whether the exclusionary rule, which is part of *Miranda*, deterred lawbreaking by the police. Even assuming that it did, he found that "sufficient deterrence flows when the evidence in question is made unavailable to the prosecution in its case in chief."

It is not immediately apparent, however, that the judicial burden has been eased by the "bright-line" rules adopted in *Miranda*. In fact, in the 34 years since *Miranda* was decided, this Court has been called upon to decide nearly 60 cases involving a host of *Miranda* issues, most of them predicted

Justice William Brennan dissented. He pointed out that the case turned on whether the jury believed Harris's version of what happened or the undercover officer's version; therefore, the impeachment evidence went to matters directly related to the charges against Harris. In contrast, *Walder* was a case in which a seizure related to a 1950 drug charge, which was dismissed on Fourth Amendment grounds, was used to impeach the defendant at a 1952 trial on different drug charges. In *Walder*, Brennan noted, the evidence used to impeach had no direct bearing on the elements of the case being tried.

Justice Brennan also contended that using a statement taken in violation of *Miranda* to impeach a defendant's testimony penalized him for taking the stand. In his view, that had the same effect as commenting to the jury on the defendant's silence—a practice the Court had earlier found unconstitutional. After criticizing the majority for in effect rewarding illegal conduct by the police, Justice Brennan expressed his concern about *Miranda*'s future: "Thus, even to the extent that *Miranda* was aimed at deterring police practices in disregard of the Constitution, I fear that today's holding will seriously undermine the achievement of that objective. . . . This [decision] goes far toward undoing much of the progress made in conforming police methods to the Constitution."

Journalist Liva Baker agreed with Justice Brennan. She observed that *Harris* marked a pronounced shift in the Court's view toward criminal justice:

> What the justices did, however, may have been more effective and in the end longer-lasting. They reversed the logic of it. . . . As Hugo Black's and Earl Warren's had been the gradually emerging judicial logic of the forties, fifties, and sixties, now ... the concerns of the dissenters to *Miranda*—were emerging as the judicial logic of the seventies.[*]

Harris was the first in a series of decisions that created exceptions to the *Miranda* rule. *Miranda* supporters argue that those decisions have stripped the rule of much of its protection of suspects.

[*]Liva Baker, *Miranda: Crime, Law, and Politics*. New York: Atheneum, 1983, p. 348.

with remarkable prescience [foresight] by Justice White in his
Miranda dissent.[75]

Some doubt whether the *Miranda* rule discourages the
police from misbehaving. As Justice John Harlan observed in
his dissent in *Miranda*, officers who use third-degree tactics and
deny it in court would do the same with *Miranda* warnings.
According to Wendy Kaminer, Justice Harlan was right:

> Police officers routinely perjure themselves to make their
> cases, New York City's Mollen Commission on police cor-
> ruption and brutality reported in 1994, to the surprise of few
> people who work in the court system. When police officers
> testify, you can sometimes see the judges suspend disbelief.
> Police regularly lie about the circumstances of arrests and
> searches to cover up Fourth Amendment violations. The
> commission found that perjury among police officers is so
> common that it has a name, "testilying."[76]

Consequently, careless and inexperienced police officers, rather
than those who act in bad faith, are most likely to run afoul of
the *Miranda* rule.

Finally, critics maintain that *Miranda* was aimed at police practices that had nearly disappeared. According to Professor Cassell,

> First, genuinely coerced confessions were, statistically speak-
> ing, rare at the time of *Miranda*. It appears to be common
> ground in the literature that, as the result of increasing
> judicial oversight and police professionalism, coercive ques-
> tioning methods began to decline in the 1930s and 1940s. By
> the 1950s, coercive questioning had, according to a leading
> scholar in the area, "diminished considerably." When the
> Supreme Court began issuing more detailed rules for police
> interrogation in the 1960s, it was dealing with a problem "that
> was already fading into the past."[77]

In other words, *Miranda* is a failed experiment in criminal justice that should be ended.

Summary

Miranda has caused serious harm to society. After the decision was handed down, the percentage of suspects who confessed to the police declined significantly and never returned to pre-*Miranda* levels. These "lost confessions" have resulted in thousands of unsolved crimes, many of them violent; guilty criminals who go free; wasted police and court time; and diminished public confidence in the justice system. *Miranda* has also done little to accomplish the Supreme Court's goal of protecting the innocent: Many guilty suspects insist on their *Miranda* rights and refuse to talk to police. Their doing so deprives the police of confessions that could clear innocent suspects.

Miranda Should Be Strengthened, Not Weakened

Both sides in the *Miranda* debate agree that about 80 percent of suspects waive their rights and submit to police
questioning—a result that neither the majority nor the dissenters in *Miranda* had expected. Professor John Taylor observed,
"The statistic does lend some support—but scant comfort—to
those who see *Miranda* as a failed initiative."[78] The high percentage of suspects who waive their rights translates into a
high percentage of suspects who confess. Journalist Alexander
Nguyen observed, "Studies suggest there has not been a decline
in the rate at which the accused make confessions; it continues
to hover at roughly 64 percent, which is what it was in the pre-
Miranda era."[79]

Citing those statistics, advocates for the rights of the accused
believe that the *Miranda* rule, as it currently exists, does not offer

adequate protection for those who are questioned while in police custody. They argue that it is time to strengthen the rule, not to scale it back further.

Miranda **did not "handcuff" the police.**

Critics of *Miranda*, Professor Paul Cassell in particular, argue that it deprives the police of a valuable crime-fighting tool and allows thousands of guilty criminals to go free. Professor Stephen Schulhofer, a law professor at the University of Chicago, reviewed the same studies that Professor Cassell used and came to a different conclusion:

> My review of the data suggests many essential qualifications that Cassell overlooks or decides to deemphasize. Some of these qualifications raise large doubts about the before-and-after studies in general; other caveats require only small changes in the magnitude of a particular estimate. But even the minor details are critical. . . . With small adjustments, the critical effects can quickly go to zero.[80]

According to Professor Schulhofer, the chief flaw in Professor Cassell's analysis was the assumption that a lost confession translated into a lost conviction—a flaw because a confession is not required for a conviction in every case. Having made that adjustment and others to the studies that Cassell relied on, Schulhofer concluded:

> Even if we accept the usefulness of before-after comparisons focused on the immediate post-*Miranda* period, the best estimate of lost convictions that such studies will support is at most a mere 0.78%, and *Miranda*'s impact on current conviction rates is almost certainly even lower. For practical purposes, *Miranda*'s empirically demonstrable harm to law enforcement is essentially nil.[81]

It has been argued that factors other than *Miranda* affected the percentage of crimes cleared by the police. During the 1960s, police resources increased only modestly while the crime rate soared. Tracking "clearance capacity"—the number of police officers assigned per 100 violent crimes reported—Professor Schulhofer found that, in 1960, 115 officers were assigned per 100 felonies, but in 1968, only 51 officers were assigned per 100 felonies. Other factors also might explain the drop in clearance rates: a shift from "acquaintance crimes" to harder-to-solve offenses committed by strangers, the overall volatility of society during the 1960s, and the poor quality of some police departments.

The Supreme Court has made *Miranda* ineffective.

President Nixon followed through on his promise to appoint "strict constructionists" to the Supreme Court. The new justices, led by Chief Justice Warren Burger, revisited the *Miranda* rule in *Harris v. New York* in 1971. They ruled that a statement taken from a defendant in violation of the *Miranda* rule could be introduced as evidence to impeach—or cast doubt on—a defendant who takes the stand in his or her own defense. Opponents of *Harris* argued that it significantly curtailed a suspect's *Miranda* rights.

Later decisions further scaled back the *Miranda* rule. They include:

- *Michigan v. Tucker* in 1974. The Court allowed a witness's testimony to be admitted at trial even though that witness had been identified through interrogation conducted in violation of the *Miranda* rule. Unlike those of a search-and-seizure violation, therefore, the "fruits" of a *Miranda* violation were admissible.

- *New York v. Quarles* in 1984. The Court recognized a "public safety" exception to the *Miranda* rule. In this case, police officers asked a suspected rapist whom they believed was armed, "Where is the gun?" before reading him his rights. The Court ruled that, in the defendant's trial for illegally possessing a gun, the lower court properly admitted his response, "The gun is over there."

- *Oregon v. Elstad* in 1985. In this case, the police obtained two statements, the first in violation of *Miranda* and the second after giving warnings. The Court ruled that the second statement should be admitted, even though the defendant thought that he had to confess because he had "let the cat out of the bag" the first time.

Some believe that these decisions have not only weakened the *Miranda* rule but also give police officers an incentive not to follow it. As Justice William Brennan remarked in his dissent in *Harris*, "This [decision] goes far toward undoing much of the progress made in conforming police methods to the Constitution."[82]

It is too easy to waive *Miranda* rights.

It has been argued that today's high confession rate, which the *Miranda* majority could not have anticipated, results from a flaw in the original rule. Some view it as a compromise. Even though a suspect is formally warned of the right to remain silent, he or she is permitted to waive those rights and confess instead. Many believe that waiver has become the exception that has swallowed up the *Miranda* rule.

One reason for widespread waivers of rights is that the right to have a lawyer present during questioning exists largely on paper. Mark Godsey, a law professor at the University of Cincinnati, explained:

Rather than waste time going through the elaborate ceremony of contacting the suspect's attorney or having an attorney appointed for her by the court, waiting while the suspect meets with her attorney, and then announces that she will no longer submit to interrogation, the police take the obvious shortcut and terminate the interrogation.[83]

Professor Godsey also suggested that suspects do not understand what the "right to remain silent" means. He explained, "Suspects may waive their rights simply because they erroneously

The "Guiding Hand" of Counsel:
Gideon v. Wainwright

One of the landmark cases that led to *Miranda* was that of *Gideon v. Wainwright*, 372 U.S. 335 (1963), which held that the Sixth Amendment's right to counsel applied to the states.

The petitioner in that case, Clarence Earl Gideon, was charged with breaking and entering, a felony. Gideon asked the trial judge to appoint a lawyer for him. Unfortunately for him, Florida was at the time one of a handful of states that appointed lawyers only in capital cases—those in which the death penalty could be imposed. Gideon represented himself, was found guilty, and was sentenced to five years in prison.

Gideon filed a petition for a writ of *habeas corpus* with the Florida Supreme Court. *Habeas corpus* is Latin for "you have the body." A writ of *habeas corpus* is a court order that commands a person who has custody of a prisoner—in Gideon's case, Louie Wainwright, the head of Florida's prison system—to bring him before the court, where it can be determined whether the prisoner is being held unlawfully.

After Florida's highest court denied his petition, Gideon asked the United States Supreme Court to review the fairness of his trial. The Court agreed to do so and, because Gideon had no funds, appointed a lawyer for him. Gideon's appointed lawyer was Abe Fortas, one of the nation's most prominent lawyers and a future justice of the Court.

The Court ruled unanimously that Florida had denied Gideon his constitutional right to counsel and reversed his conviction. In doing so, it overruled *Betts v. Brady*, (1942), which held that the Sixth Amendment did not apply to the states. Justice Hugo Black, who wrote the majority opinion in *Gideon*, bluntly stated, "the Court conclude that remaining silent 'looks bad' and will ultimately hurt their chances in court, basing their decision on a set of warnings that has not caught up with the law."[84] The *Miranda* warnings do nothing to dispel the belief that silence will be commented on in court—or worse.

Finally, *Miranda* has done little to dispel the secrecy that surrounds police interrogation of suspects. Professor Yale Kamisar, one of *Miranda*'s strongest supporters, wrote, "We know little

in *Betts* was wrong." Noting the importance of having a lawyer at one's trial, Justice Black wrote, "[That the] government hires lawyers to prosecute and defendants who have the money hire lawyers to defend are the strongest indications of the widespread belief that lawyers in criminal courts are necessities, not luxuries."

Although the vote was unanimous, the concurring opinions showed that the justices were divided as to whether the entire Bill of Rights applied to the states through the due process clause of the Fourteenth Amendment. Justice William O. Douglas expressed his belief that it did. (Justice Hugo Black had also long held that view.) Justice John Harlan rejected the notion that the entire Bill of Rights applied to the states, however. His argument rested in part on federalism—that is, the division of power between the federal and state governments:

> I do not read our past decisions to suggest that, by so holding, we automatically carry over an entire body of federal law and apply it in full sweep to the States. Any such concept would disregard the frequently wide disparity between the legitimate interests of the States and of the Federal Government, the divergent problems that they face, and the significantly different consequences of their actions.

Gideon involved a right considered so important that the justices took the unusual step of giving it retroactive effect. That ruling forced the state of Florida to either retry or set free hundreds of inmates in its prison system.

more about actual police interrogation practices than we did at the time of *Miranda*."[85] When he was on the Supreme Court, Justice William O. Douglas found disturbing parallels between police interrogation in the United States and the justice system in the former Soviet Union:

> In [Russia] detention incommunicado is the common practice, and the period of permissible detention now extends for nine months. Where there is custodial interrogation, it is clear that the critical stage of the trial takes place long before the courtroom formalities commence. That is apparent to one who attends criminal trials in Russia. Those that I viewed never put in issue the question of guilt; guilt was an issue resolved in the inner precincts of a prison under questioning by the police.[86]

Miranda has not ended coercion.

By the time the Supreme Court heard *United States v. Dickerson*, the law-enforcement community had learned to live with the *Miranda* rule, especially since it had been scaled back over the years. It was therefore no surprise that relatively few law-enforcement groups joined the effort to overturn *Miranda*. John Taylor explained the change of heart:

> [The] police have learned to pressure or cajole suspects into waiving their rights and then to interrogate them aggressively using deception and manipulative psychological techniques, and the courts now tend to presume the voluntariness of confessions when the formalities of warning and waiver have been observed. The consequence, these critics suggest, is that in some respects suspects under interrogation today have less protection than they had previously under the due process standard alone. It is no wonder that police now generally support *Miranda*.[87]

It has been argued that *Miranda* merely shifted the focus from coercing suspects to incriminate themselves to coercing them to waive their rights. Once the police obtain a waiver that will stand up in court, they are free to use almost any tactic short of physical or psychological torture. In a 1992 article entitled "The Ethics of Deceptive Interrogation," Professors Richard Leo and Jerome Skolnick listed some of the deceptive tactics commonly used by the police to deceive suspects. They include the following:

- Describing the questioning as an "interview" and telling the suspect that he or she is free to leave, thus making the encounter "noncustodial."

- Delivering the *Miranda* warnings in a matter-of-fact tone of voice so as to minimize their significance.

- Misrepresenting the nature of the offense or the facts of the case.

- Appealing to the suspect's conscience and making the interrogation seem less adversarial than it is.

- Downplaying the moral seriousness of the offense, for example, suggesting to a rape suspect that "she was asking for it."

- Indirectly promising leniency in exchange for a confession.

- Misrepresenting one's identity, for example, a police officer posing as a fellow prison inmate.

- Confronting the suspect with false evidence of guilt, such as lying to him or her that an accomplice has confessed or telling him that he failed a lie-detector test.

Professors Leo and Skolnick observed,

in these deception cases, we do not usually encounter prudent suspects who are skeptical of the police. Such suspects rarely, if ever, waive their constitutional rights to silence or to an attorney. As in many deception cases, the suspect, young or old, white or black, has naively waived his right to remain silent and to an attorney.[88]

Liva Baker recounted a story that shows how little protection the *Miranda* rule offers:

Miranda gave no protection from police overbearing to Peter Reilly of New Canaan, Connecticut, accused of murdering his mother. Police carefully advised him of his rights, and eighteen-year-old Peter, unacquainted with the ways of law enforcement, turned down the offer of a lawyer and asked instead for a lie detector test, after which police viciously and deliberately manipulated him into confessing. . . . Ultimately the charges were dropped when new evidence placed Reilly miles from the scene of the crime at the time it had occurred.

The *Miranda* ruling itself held inherent weaknesses; the major one was that it allowed a suspect to waive his rights without the advice of a lawyer. A lawyer would never have allowed what happened to Peter Reilly.[89]

Baker added that this miscarriage of justice was remedied only because strong public interest in the case, including the involvement of playwright Arthur Miller, prodded the police to investigate further.

False confessions are still a serious problem.

Not only do most suspects waive their *Miranda* rights and confess, but, as the case of Peter Reilly illustrates, some confess to crimes that they did not commit. This may be difficult to believe—common sense leads to the conclusion that innocent people do not confess—but it appears to happen often. In 1986,

Professor C. Ronald Huff, now at the University of California, Irvine, conservatively estimated that 6,000 people per year were wrongly convicted of serious crimes. Other studies have shown

Proposed New *Miranda* Warnings

Mark Godsey, a law professor at the University of Cincinnati, has concluded that the *Miranda* rule did not stop the police from using coercion to obtain confessions from suspects. In a recent law review article, Professor Godsey offered his proposal for revised *Miranda* warnings that, in his opinion, would be more effective.[*]

Introductory Remarks

You have a number of important constitutional rights that protect you when law enforcement officers ask questions of you. These rights ensure that police interviews are conducted in a civilized and humane manner and that, if you talk, it is a choice made by you of your own free will.

The Right to Remain Silent

First and foremost, you have a right to remain silent. This means, of course, that you do not have to talk to us.

Implications of Remaining Silent

If you choose to remain silent at the beginning or at any time during the interview, you will not be penalized in any way for doing so. You will not be physically harmed or punished, you will not be deprived of any benefits or privileges, and your silence will not be used against you in court to suggest that you have something to hide and must therefore be guilty.

Implications of Talking

If you choose to talk, anything you say will be used against you in a court of law. If you choose to talk, you may change your mind and remain silent at any time. In other words, we will honor your request to remain silent at any time, and this interview will last no longer than you wish it to last. We also, as required by law, have already started videotaping our entire interview with you, and this tape will be admissible in a court of law by you or by law enforcement to prove what was said and what happened during this interview.

[*]Mark A. Godsey, "Reformulating the *Miranda* Warnings in Light of Contemporary Law and Understandings." MINN. L. REV. 90(4): 781, 813 (2006).

a false-confession rate somewhere between 14 and 25 percent. It can be argued, therefore, that thousands of Americans are behind bars for crimes that they did not commit.

Some innocent people have been sentenced to death. David Dow, a Texas lawyer who has represented death-row inmates, remarked, "Far from being foolproof evidence of guilt, confessions are common even in cases where the suspect is unquestionably innocent."[90] Dow pointed out that more than 140 prisoners have been exonerated on the basis of DNA evidence. In other words, they were convicted, sentenced, and sent to prison for a crime that science has since proved that someone else committed. More than 20 percent of those men signed confessions.

One reason this happens is that interrogators' minds are already made up. As Gary Stuart explained, "If a suspect is in custodial interrogation rather than a mere witness interview, detectives already believe they have the right man sitting at the table in front of them."[91] That frame of mind can have serious consequences. One example, mentioned by John Stuart, was the investigation of a mass murder at a Buddhist temple in his home state of Arizona. In that case, the police obtained six confessions after obtaining waivers of the defendants' *Miranda* rights. Four of those confessions turned out to be "indisputably false." Stuart remarked, "The motive or the psychological explanation for the confessions by the Tucson Four may never be known, but in acknowledgment that such false confessions do occur, and not infrequently, the criminal justice system must be skeptical of all confessions."[92]

Richard Leo and co-author Richard Ofshe, a sociology professor at the University of California, Berkeley, added that, in high-profile cases such as that of the Tucson Four, the police who coerced confessions from innocent parties in the first place did everything they could to discredit the later, true confessions. Such behavior makes miscarriages of justice even more likely.

Summary

In spite of the Supreme Court's good intentions, *Miranda* has not adequately protected suspects from coercive interrogation. The *Miranda* rule was flawed from the beginning because it was too easy for the police to persuade suspects to waive their constitutional rights. Later decisions further scaled back *Miranda*'s protection. As a result, false confessions and the wrongful convictions that result from them remain serious problems. By the time the Supreme Court revisited *Miranda* in *Dickerson v. United States*, the *Miranda* rule had become so weak that both the police and the Court could afford to "live with" it.

The Future of *Miranda*

Many believe that, by 2000, when *Dickerson v. United States* reaffirmed *Miranda*, the Supreme Court and the law-enforcement community had come to terms with the *Miranda* rule—and with each other. *Dickerson* has been described as the Court's "last word" on *Miranda*. Nevertheless, the *Miranda* rule still has enormous cultural significance and remains a lightning rod in the debate over larger issues such as the proper role of judges, the balance between liberty and security, and the meaning of the Bill of Rights.

Whether or not *Miranda* remains law, as long as the police rely on confessions to prove guilt, there will be debate as to whether suspects ever voluntarily confess. John Taylor observed,

> For all the controversy about *Miranda*, the fundamental questions, both before and after waiver, thus continue to be the same ones that vexed the Court prior to 1966: what sorts of

94

pressure on suspects are tolerable, how much pressure on suspects is too much pressure, and how are police to be held to the standards we adopt?[93]

Has *Miranda* Been Given Eternal Life?

Since the Rehnquist Court not only reaffirmed *Miranda* but described the *Miranda* rule as constitutional in nature, it has been suggested that the decision has become a "superprecedent," one that is likely to stand no matter who is on the Supreme Court. According to Jeffrey Rosen, a law professor at George Washington University:

> The term superprecedents first surfaced at the Supreme Court confirmation hearings of Judge John Roberts, when Senator Arlen Specter of Pennsylvania, the chairman of the Judiciary Committee, asked him whether he agreed that certain cases like *Roe [v. Wade]* had become superprecedents or "super-duper" precedents—that is, that they were so deeply embedded in the fabric of law they should be especially hard to overturn.[94]

Rosen quoted Daniel Farber, a law professor at the University of California, Berkeley, who commented on the surprising power of *stare decisis*:

> If somebody had told me in 1968 that Republicans would make all but two of the Supreme Court appointments of the next 37 years and at the end of that time, *Miranda* would still be on the books, there would be a constitutional right to abortion, and all the Warren court's major decisions would still be there, I never would have believed it.[95]

Still, it is not out of the question that the Court might someday overturn *Miranda*, for several reasons. One is that future justices might have an entirely different conception of what the Bill of Rights means. The legal philosophy of Justice Antonin

(continued on page 98)

Miranda Reaffirmed: *Dickerson v. United States*

In 1968, Congress reacted to *Miranda* by adding Title 18, §3501, to the United States Code. This imposed a voluntariness standard for confessions. Supporters claimed that the legislation was not an effort to overrule *Miranda*, because the Supreme Court had invited Congress and the states to develop alternatives to the *Miranda* rule.

Section 3501 lay dormant for years. Then, opponents of *Miranda* finally found a case in which the defendant had confessed voluntarily but had not been given the *Miranda* warnings. The defendant, Charles Dickerson, was convicted of bank robbery, conspiracy to commit bank robbery, and using a gun while committing a violent crime. His statement led police to the actual robber, Jimmy Rochester, as well as to evidence that Dickerson was an accomplice.

The trial court suppressed Dickerson's confession. The government appealed the ruling to the United States Court of Appeals for the Fourth Circuit. Because Dickerson's confession was crucial to the case, the Fourth Circuit heard the appeal even though the trial had not yet occurred. It also took the unusual step of giving two organizations that wanted *Miranda* overturned *amicus curiae* status—that is, it allowed them to submit legal arguments even though they were not parties to the case. Both organizations argued that Dickerson's confession should be admitted because it was "voluntary" within the meaning of §3501. The appeals court agreed.

The Justice Department appealed to the Supreme Court. Author John Taylor explained what was at stake:

> The issue was clear. If the *Miranda* decision established constitutional rights, then Congress had no power to overturn it, for the Supreme Court is the ultimate interpreter of the Constitution and its interpretations can be overturned only by constitutional amendment. If, on the other hand, *Miranda* merely announced judicially created rules of evidence, then Congress could revise those rules for the federal courts, and the *Miranda* rules would not bind the states, either, for the Supreme Court has no supervisory administrative authority over the rules and procedures of state courts.[*]

Many observers thought that the Court was prepared to overrule *Miranda*.

In *Dickerson v. United States*, 530 U.S. 428 (2000), however, the justices voted 7 to 2 to reaffirm *Miranda*. Chief Justice Rehnquist, who strongly condemned *Miranda* earlier in his career, wrote the majority opinion. He found that §3501 was an attempt to legislatively overrule *Miranda*. He observed, "Given §3501's express designation of voluntariness as the touchstone of admissibility, its omission of any warning requirement, and the instruction for trial courts to consider a nonexclusive list of factors relevant to the circumstances of a confession, we agree with the Court of Appeals that Congress intended by its enactment to overrule *Miranda*.**

The chief justice next concluded that the *Miranda* rule was based on the Constitution and not a mere rule of evidence. He went on to conclude that §3501 was not an appropriate alternative to the *Miranda* rule but instead an attempt to do away with it.

Finally, even if *Miranda* was wrongly decided in the first place, the chief justice concluded that the principle of *stare decisis* weighed against overruling it so many years later. Although *stare decisis* was not an inflexible rule, some "special justification" was required to overturn an earlier decision. He concluded, "We do not think there is such justification for overruling *Miranda. Miranda* has become embedded in routine police practice to the point where the warnings have become part of our national culture."

Justice Antonin Scalia dissented. He criticized the majority for concluding in earlier cases that the *Miranda* rule was not based on the Constitution but now arguing the opposite position. He also accused the majority of writing "prophylactic" restrictions on Congress and the states into the Constitution and, in doing so, exercising power not given by the Framers. Justice Scalia went on to assert that *Miranda* was wrongly decided in the first place. He wrote that "any conclusion that a violation of the *Miranda* rules necessarily amounts to a violation of the privilege against compelled self-incrimination can claim no support in history, precedent, or common sense."

Finally, Justice Scalia rejected the argument that *Miranda* should survive because of its special place in the public's consciousness. He wrote:

> I believe we cannot allow to remain on the books even a celebrated decision—especially a celebrated decision—that has come to stand for the proposition that the Supreme Court has power to impose extraconstitutional constraints upon Congress and the States. This is not the system that was established by the Framers, or that would be established by any sane supporter of government by the people.

*John B. Taylor, *The Right to Counsel and the Privilege Against Self-Incrimination.* Santa Barbara, CA: ABC-CLIO, Inc., 2004, p. 222.
**530 U.S. 428, 436

(continued from page 95)

Scalia—that the Constitution must be interpreted according to its "common sense" meaning—rejects the *Miranda* rule because there is nothing to indicate that the Framers intended such a standard to exist. It is also possible that the pendulum will swing away from federal power and back toward states' rights, reversing at least some of the "due process revolution" of the 1960s. Alternatively, a future Court might decide that the *Miranda* rule has outlived its usefulness and could truly allow states to experiment with alternatives. As Justice William O. Douglas wrote during the "due process revolution," "Happily, all constitutional questions are always open."[96]

Another possibility is that the *Miranda* rule and other protections that our system currently affords to suspects will be swept away if this country suffers another large-scale terrorist attack. After the September 11, 2001, attacks, Congress passed the far-reaching USA Patriot Act, which expanded the power of federal law-enforcement agencies and reduced the courts' authority to oversee them. Many legal analysts believe that future attacks will result in laws that are even more sweeping than the Patriot Act. They also believe that the courts will uphold them as valid wartime measures, just as they upheld harsh prison sentences for antiwar activists during World War I and the internment of Japanese Americans during World War II. In his book *All Laws But One*, Chief Justice Rehnquist wrote, "In time of war a nation may be required to respond to a condition without making a careful inquiry as to how that condition came about."[97]

If *Miranda* Fell, What Would Happen?

Even if the Court does not overrule *Miranda* outright, some observers believe that the Court's post-*Dickerson* decisions have further eroded an already weak *Miranda* rule. Those decisions also suggest that *Miranda* is in fact on shaky legal ground.

What would happen if *Miranda* fell? First, the Supreme Court would go back to deciding confession cases under the pre-*Miranda* voluntariness standard. Perhaps §3501 finally would become good law. Some scholars believe that such a development would be a healthy one. They contend that the *Miranda* rule has allowed the police to "go through the motions" of advising suspects of their rights and has actually discouraged the courts from exploring whether confessions obtained through the use of modern psychological tactics are in fact voluntary.

The end of *Miranda* will not necessarily mean the end of *Miranda*-like procedures at the state level. Some states will continue to require them as part of their law, either under the state constitution or through legislation. Even if *Miranda*-like procedures are not required, police officials may continue to require them as best departmental practice or as a means to avoid lawsuits or losing convictions on appeal. When *Dickerson* was argued before the Supreme Court, the FBI informed the justices that its agents would continue to provide *Miranda*-like warnings regardless of how they ruled—just as the agency did during the 14 years before *Miranda*.

Is it Time to Rewrite the *Miranda* Rule?

Professor Mark Godsey used the occasion of the fortieth anniversary of *Miranda* to review the *Miranda* rule. He concluded that much of the rule has become obsolete: "Empirical research and four decades of practical experience have demonstrated that the warnings do not fully achieve their intended policy objectives. The legal rights embodied in the warnings have been altered, with new rights being recognized while others have fallen into the background."[98]

According to Godsey, the *Miranda* rule's principal shortcoming is that it does not explicitly tell the suspect what will happen if he or she chooses not to talk. Most people are unaware that the prosecutor or the judge cannot penalize a defendant who remains silent. Godsey suggested,

> Rather than leaving the suspect guessing as to what a 'right to remain silent' means, the warnings should adequately explain,

in plain language, what it means to say that her choice to remain silent is a 'right.' She will not be tortured, she will not lose benefits or privileges, and her silence will not be used against her in court.[99]

Godsey also proposed "refresher" warnings to ensure that the suspect's will is not overcome during a lengthy interrogation:

> A rule could be easily constructed that would require the police to obtain a written waiver of the right to remain silent, for example, at the beginning of each hour of interrogation. The suspect and the interrogator would sign the waiver form at the beginning of the interrogation, and each would place their initials next to the time of day at each interval at which the re-recitation of the rights took place.[100]

Justice Byron White, who dissented in *Miranda*, suggested "specific time limits, tailored to fit the cause."[101]

Is Videotaping Confessions the Solution?

Video technology is so inexpensive that Americans routinely record birthday parties and a growing number of people carry cell phones with recording capability. With that technology so widely available, people on both sides of the *Miranda* debate—including, for example, Professors Cassell and Godsey—have called for the recording of interrogations. Advocates of law enforcement believe that recording interrogations would enable detectives to concentrate on the suspect rather than take notes, enable police departments to identify and discipline rogue officers, and use recordings to teach proper interrogation techniques. They add that recording would discourage trumped-up charges of coercion and police brutality, eliminate baseless motions and appeals, and make it easier for jurors to notice when a suspect "made up a story as he went along."

At the same time, those in favor of suspects' rights believe that recording would discourage coercion because the camera would serve as an "independent witness" to police misconduct in much the same way as having a defense lawyer present. They

New Jersey's Rule on Recording of Interrogations

New Jersey's Criminal Rule 3:17 was the result of a decision by that state's supreme court, *State v. Cook*, 179 N.J. 533, 847 A.2d 530 (Sup. Ct. 2004). In *Cook*, the court rejected the defendant's argument that due process of law required the police to record his interrogation. The justices did announce, however, that they would create a special committee to study the issue of recording custodial interrogations.

After studying the experience of states that had adopted some form of recording requirement, the committee recommended that the state supreme court impose a recording requirement as a rule of evidence. The court adopted the committee's recommendations as Rule 3:17.

Subsection (a) of the rule requires that custodial interrogations conducted in a place of detention be recorded if the person being interrogated is being charged with one of the serious crimes listed in the rule.

Subsection (b) of the rule lists exceptions to the recording requirement:

- Recording is not feasible.

- The suspect made a spontaneous statement or responded to routine questions that are asked during the processing of people who have been arrested.

- The suspect refused to have the interrogation recorded.

- The interrogation was held out of state.

- The suspect was interrogated for a crime not covered by the rule.

The prosecution has the burden of proving that an exception applies.

If the prosecution intends to claim an exception to the rule, subsection (c) requires it to notify the court and to furnish the defense with the names of the witnesses whom it will call regarding the defendant's statement. It also requires the court to hold a hearing to determine whether the exception applies.

Subsection (d) provides that failure by the police to record an interrogation "shall be a factor for consideration" by the judge in determining whether to admit the defendant's statement and by the jury in determining how much weight, if any, to give to the statement.

If the prosecution introduces a statement that is covered by this rule but was not recorded, subsection (e) requires the judge to instruct the jury regarding how much weight it should give such a statement.

The rule took effect January 1, 2006, for homicide cases and was extended to all other offenses covered by the rule effective January 1, 2007.

also believe that recording confessions causes less of a "swearing contest" that heavily favors the police and allows jurors to hear incriminating statements in the defendant's own words rather than the version "spun" by the police.

There is growing support for recording within the legal community. In 1985, in *Stephan v. State*, Alaska's highest court held that recording of confessions was required as a matter of due process. At least six other states and the District of Columbia have followed Alaska's lead and imposed some form of record-ing requirement. These requirements vary as to the offenses to which they apply and the admissibility of an unrecorded state-ment. More states may follow this example. Section 130.4 of the American Law Institute's Model Code of Pre-Arraignment Pro-cedure requires that a sound recording be made of the *Miranda* warnings and "any questioning of the arrested person and any statement he makes in response thereto." The Model Code also provides that a defendant's statement may be suppressed when there was a "substantial violation" of the recording requirement.

Still, most states have not moved to require the recording of confessions. One reason is caution. Perhaps mindful of the unintended consequences of *Miranda*, courts and legislatures have moved cautiously. There is, however, another reason: Some police departments would rather operate in secret. Professor Yale Kamisar observed:

> A few years ago, when it was disclosed that some Chicago police officers had been torturing suspects into confess-ing, the Illinois Legislature seemed prepared to enact a law requiring video or audiotaping of police interrogations, but that bill died under opposition from the law-enforce-ment community, which claimed the law would expand the rights of the accused at the expense of public safety. Why making a complete record of what happened during inter-rogations would expand the rights of the accused was not made clear.[102]

Other Proposals

Susan Klein, a law professor at the University of Texas at Austin, believes that the lack of legal remedies available to a person interrogated in violation of the *Miranda* rule has gutted *Miranda*. Klein wrote, "Today's Court, by severely limiting the remedies available for violations of the Self-Incrimination Clause and the *Miranda* warnings, not only permits officers to ignore both but actually encourages their violation."[103] She believes that a person who was wrongly interrogated should be allowed to file suit against the offending police department under federal civil-rights laws. The trend appears to be one of narrowing, not broadening, the right to sue, however. In *Chavez v. Martinez*, the Supreme Court indicated that it would be very difficult to win a lawsuit that was based on a *Miranda* rule violation.

Charles Ogletree, a law professor at Harvard, has argued in favor of a rule that would prohibit the police from interrogating a suspect at all until he or she has first talked to a lawyer:

> If, after conferring with counsel, a suspect desires to make a statement, it may be used against her. Any statements made without the assistance of counsel, however, would be inadmissible. . . . This solution completes the *Miranda* Court's effort to reconcile conflicting doctrine on confessions in a way that maintains this nation's commitment to an accusatorial rather than an inquisitorial system of criminal justice, and reaffirms the constitutional values that motivated the decision.[104]

Ogletree believes that, without a rule this sweeping, there is no meaningful protection of the suspect's right to remain silent.

Akhil Amar, a law professor at Yale University, believes that interrogation should take place in open court rather than in the police station. Professor Amar explained:

> Questioning would be accomplished in a relatively civilized setting, as in civil litigation, rather than in the rough-and-tumble

atmosphere of interrogation at the police station, with its atten-
dant intimidation, sleeplessness, and other physical and psychological pressures. The process would be judicially supervised;
refusals to answer and outright lies would be punished with
judicial contempt or adverse inferences, not with fists banging
on desks and shouted four-letter words. These depositions and
hearings would act as the modern equivalent of the nineteenth-
century questioning of the accused by a magistrate.[105]

Gary Stuart suggested that the debate over confessions might
become less relevant as police become less reliant on them:

> Open meeting laws, public records legislation, and "sunshine"
> budgets may motivate the executive branch to the point that
> confessions are not the mainstay of police work. Also, DNA
> testing, vastly improved fingerprinting, and crime scene
> forensics are already producing physical evidence that can
> supersede eyewitness testimony and even the suspect's own
> admissions of guilt. It likely will come to pass that the map-
> ping of the human genome and further advancements in
> DNA testing will change both the methodology and the law
> of confessions.[106]

In the meantime, however, the police use confessions to
clear thousands of crimes per year, the law of confessions continues to evolve, and the controversy over them goes on.

Summary

Although *Dickerson* appears to have ended the *Miranda* debate,
it is possible that the Supreme Court will either overrule
Miranda or replace it with a different standard. If *Miranda* were
overruled, confessions would be governed by the voluntariness

standard, although many states and localities would continue to offer suspects *Miranda*-like protection. Legal experts on both sides of the debate have proposed alternatives to *Miranda*. The proposal with the most support is a requirement that the police record interrogations. A growing number of jurisdictions are imposing such a requirement.

NOTES ///////

Introduction: *Miranda v. Arizona*

1 Gary L. Stuart, *Miranda: The Story of America's Right to Remain Silent*. Tucson: University of Arizona Press, 2004, p. 6.

2 Ibid., pp. 6–7.

3 John B. Taylor, *The Right to Counsel and the Privilege Against Self-Incrimination*. Santa Barbara, CA: ABC-CLIO, Inc., 2004, pp. 158–159.

4 U.S. Const. amend. VI.

5 U.S. Const. amend V.

6 *Miranda v. Arizona*, 384 U.S. 436, 457–458 (1966).

7 *Miranda v. Arizona*, 384 U.S. 436, 455 (1966).

8 *Miranda v. Arizona*, 384 U.S. 436, 458 (1966).

9 *Dickerson v. United States*, 530 U.S. 428, 443 (2000).

Point: *Miranda* Was Wrongly Decided and Should Be Overruled

10 Liva Baker, *Miranda: Crime, Law, and Politics*. New York: Atheneum, 1983, p. 27.

11 530 U.S. 428, 461 (Scalia, J., dissenting).

12 Robert E. Precht, *Defending Mohammed: Justice on Trial*. Ithaca, NY: Cornell University Press, 2003, p. 129.

13 *Miranda v. Arizona*, 384 U.S. 436, 526 (1966) (White, J., dissenting).

14 *Escobedo v. Illinois*, 378 U.S. 478, 493–494 (1964) (Stewart, J., dissenting).

15 *Escobedo v. Illinois*, 378 U.S. 478, 495 (1964) (White, J., dissenting).

16 Baker, *Miranda*, p. 101.

17 Ibid., p. 195.

18 *Dickerson v. United States*, 530 U.S. 428, 464-65 (2000) (Scalia, J., dissenting).

19 Stuart, *Miranda*, p. 82.

20 Paul G. Cassell, "The Guilty and the 'Innocent': An Examination of Alleged Cases of Wrongful Conviction From False Confessions," HARV. J.L. & PUB. POL'Y 22(2): 523, 599 (Spring 1999).

21 *Miranda v. Arizona*, 384 U.S. 436, 524 (1966) (Harlan, J., dissenting).

22 Baker, *Miranda*, p. 19.

Counterpoint: *Miranda* Is Consistent With the Bill of Rights

23 Stuart, *Miranda*, p. 29.

24 Richard A. Leo, "The Impact of *Miranda* Revisited," J. CRIM. L. & CRIMINOLOGY 86(3): 621, 629 (Spring 1996).

25 Baker, *Miranda*, p. 67.

26 *Miranda v. Arizona*, 384 U.S. 436, 455 (1966).

27 *Powell v. Alabama*, 287 U.S. 45, 69 (1932).

28 *The King v. Warickshall*, 1 Leach 262, 263-264, 168 Eng. Rep. 234, 235 (K.B. 1783).

29 Stuart, *Miranda*, p. 154.

30 *Escobedo v. Illinois*, 378 U.S. 478, 486 (1964).

31 Stuart, *Miranda*, p. 140.

32 Baker, *Miranda* p. 106.

33 Taylor, *The Right to Counsel*, p. 187.

34 Stuart, *Miranda*, pp. 120–121.

35 *Mapp v. Ohio*, 367 U.S. 643, 659 (1961).

Point: Given Today's Crime Problem, *Miranda* Is Inappropriate

36 *Miranda v. Arizona*, 384 U.S. 436, 542-43 (White, J., dissenting).

37 384 U.S. 436, 441, footnote 3. The quote is from the May 14, 1965, *New York Times*.

38 Taylor, *The Right to Counsel*, p. 268.

39 Paul G. Cassell, *Handcuffing the Cops:* Miranda*'s Harmful Effects on Law Enforcement*. Policy Report No. 218. Dallas, TX: National Center for Policy Analysis, 1998, p. 14. Also available online at ncpa.org.

40 Baker, *Miranda*, p. 37.

41 Paul Cassell and Stephen J. Markman, "Miranda's Hidden Costs," *National Review*. 47(24) (December 25, 1995), p. 30.

42 *Miranda v. Arizona*, 384 U.S. 436, 537, 539 (1966) (White, J., dissenting).

43 Stuart, *Miranda* p. 148.

44 *Miranda v. Arizona*, 384 U.S. 436, 538 (1966) (White, J., dissenting).

45 *Miranda v. Arizona*, 384 U.S. 436, 517 (1966) (Harlan, J., dissenting).

46 Bruce Fein, "Miranda Handcuffs Police Even When the Danger to Civil Liberties

106

Is Marginal." *Insight on the News*, May 15, 2000.

47 Baker, *Miranda*, p. 246.

48 Wendy Kaminer, *It's All the Rage: Crime and Culture*. Reading, MA: Addison-Wesley, 1995, p. 160.

49 Ibid., p. 178.

Counterpoint: The *Miranda* Rule Encourages Civilized Police Behavior

50 Baker, *Miranda*, p. 13.

51 Taylor, *The Right to Counsel*, p. 268.

52 Stuart, *Miranda*, pp. xx–xxi.

53 Ibid., p. xv.

54 *Miranda v. Arizona*, 384 U.S. 436, 457–458 (1966).

55 Taylor, *The Right to Counsel* p. 37.

56 *Escobedo v. Illinois,* 378 U.S. 478, 489 (1964).

57 J. Edgar Hoover, "Civil Liberties and Law Enforcement: The Role of the FBI." Iowa L. Rev. 37(2): 175, 177, 179 (1952).

58 Richard A. Leo and Jerome H. Skolnick, "The Ethics of Deceptive Interrogation." *Criminal Justice Ethics.* 11(1): (Winter/Spring 1992): 312.

59 *Chavez v. Martinez*, 538 U.S. 760, 801 (2003) (Ginsberg, J., dissenting in part).

60 *Miranda v. Arizona*, 384 U.S. 436, 481 (1966).

61 Baker, *Miranda*, p. 406.

62 Hoover, "Civil Liberties," Iowa L. Rev., pp. 175, 177.

Point: *Miranda* Has Hindered the Fight Against Crime

63 Alexander Nguyen, "The Assault on *Miranda*," *The American Prospect.* 11(10) (March 27–April 10, 2000). Also available online at http://www.prospect.org/print-friendly/print/V11/10/nguyen-a.html.

64 Paul G. Cassell, "Miranda's Social Costs: An Empirical Reassessment." Nw. U. L. Rev. 90(2): 391 (Winter 1996).

65 Cassell and Markman, "The *Miranda* Rule," *National Review*, p. 30.

66 Cassell, *Handcuffing the Cops*, p. 3.

67 Ibid., p. 14.

68 Fein, "*Miranda* Handcuffs Police," *Insight on the News*, May 15, 2000.

69 Cassell and Markman, "*Miranda*'s Hidden Costs," *National Review*, p. 30.

70 Cassell, "The Guilty and the 'Innocent,'" Harv. J.L. & Pub. Pol'y, pp. 523, 526

71 Ibid., p. 532.

72 *Miranda v. Arizona*, 384 U.S. 436, 470 (1966).

73 Baker, *Miranda*, pp. 283–284.

74 *Miranda v. Arizona*, 384 U.S. 436, 545 (1966) (White, J., dissenting).

75 *Dickerson v. United States*, 530 U.S. 428, 463 (2000) (Scalia, J., dissenting).

76 Kaminer, *It's All the Rage,* p. 89.

77 Cassell, *Handcuffing the Cops,* pp. 15–16.

Counterpoint: *Miranda* Should Be Strengthened, Not Weakened

78 Taylor, *The Right to Counsel*, p. 244.

79 Nguyen, "The Assault on *Miranda*," http://www.prospect.org/print-friendly/print/V11/10/nguyen-a.html.

80 Stephen J. Schulhofer, "*Miranda*'s Practical Effect: Substantial Benefits and Vanishingly Small Social Costs." Nw. U. L. Rev. 90(2): 503, 505 (Winter 1996).

81 Ibid., p. 506.

82 *Harris v. New York*, 401 U.S. 222, 232 (1971) (Brennan, J., dissenting).

83 Mark A. Godsey, "Reformulating the *Miranda* Warnings in Light of Contemporary Law and Understandings." Minn. L. Rev. 90(4): 781, 797–798 (2006).

84 Ibid., pp. 784–785.

85 Yale Kamisar, "Interrogating Suspects: Limit Police Secrecy." *National Law Journal*, July 9, 2003. National Association of Criminal Defense Lawyers. http://www.nacdl.org/sl_docs.nsf/freeform/Mandatory:151?OpenDocument.

86 *Coleman v. Alabama*, 399 U.S. 1, 15–16 (1970) (Douglas, J., concurring).

87 Taylor, *The Right to Counsel,* p. 243.

88 Leo and Skolnick, "The Ethics of Deceptive Interrogation," *Criminal Justice Ethics.* 11(1) (Winter/Spring 1992): 3.

89 Baker, *Miranda*, p. 408.

90 David Dow, *Executed on a Technicality: Lethal Injustice on America's Death Row.* Boston, MA: Beacon Books, 2005, pp. 97–98.

91 Stuart, *Miranda*, p. 90.

92 Ibid., p. 158–159.

Conclusion: The Future of *Miranda*

93 Taylor, *The Right to Counsel,* p. 244.

94 Jeffrey Rosen, "So, Do You Believe in 'Superprecedent'?," *New York Times,* October 30, 2005.

95 Ibid.

96 *Gideon v. Wainwright,* 372 U.S. 335, 346 (1963) (Douglas, J., concurring).

97 William H. Rehnquist, *All Laws But One: Civil Liberties in Wartime.* New York, NY: Alfred A. Knopf, 1998, p. 207.

98 Godsey, "Reformulating the Miranda Warnings," MINN. L. REV. 90(4): 781, 825.

99 Ibid. pp. 814–815.

100 Ibid., p. 807.

101 384 U.S. 436, 535 (1966) (White, J., dissenting).

102 Yale Kamisar, "Interrogating Suspects," http://www.nacdl.org/sl_docs.nsf/freeform/Mandatory:151?OpenDocument.

103 Susan R. Klein, "*Miranda* Deconstitutionalized: When the Self-Incrimination Clause and the Civil Rights Act Collide." U. PA. L. REV., 143(2):417, 457 (December 1994).

104 Charles J. Ogletree, "Are Confessions Really Good for the Soul? A Proposal to Mirandize *Miranda*." HARV. L. REV. 100(7):1826, 1830–1831.

105 Akhil Reed Amar, *The Constitution and Criminal Procedure: First Principles.* New Haven, CT: Yale University Press, 1997, p. 87.

106 Stuart, *Miranda,* p. 172.

Books and Articles

Baker, Liva. *Miranda: Crime, Law, and Politics.* New York: Atheneum, 1983.

Cassell, Paul G. "The Guilty and the 'Innocent': An Examination of Wrongful Conviction From False Confessions," Harv. J.L. Publ. Pol'y 22(2):523 (Spring 1999).

———. *Handcuffing the Cops:* Miranda's *Harmful Effects on Law Enforcement.* Policy Report No. 218. Dallas, TX: National Center for Policy Analysis, 1998. Also available at http://www.ncpa.org.

———. "*Miranda*'s Social Costs: An Empirical Reassessment." Nw. L. Rev. 90(2): 391 (Winter 1996).

Godsey, Mark A. "Reformulating the *Miranda* Warnings in Light of Contemporary Law and Understandings." Minn. L. Rev. 90(4):781 (April 2006).

Leo, Richard A. "The Impact of *Miranda* Revisited." J Crim. L. & Criminology 86(3):621 (Spring 1996).

Leo, Richard A., and Jerome H. Skolnick. "The Ethics of Deceptive Interrogation." Criminal Justice Ethics 11(1):3 (Winter/Spring 1992).

Schulhofer, Stephen J. "*Miranda*'s Practical Effect: Substantial Benefits and Vanishingly Small Social Costs." Nw. L. Rev. 90(2):503 (Winter 1996).

Stuart, Gary L. *Miranda: The Story of America's Right to Remain Silent.* Tucson: University of Arizona Press, 2004.

Taylor, John B. *The Right to Counsel and the Privilege Against Self-Incrimination.* Santa Barbara, CA: ABC-CLIO, Inc., 2004.

RESOURCES ///////

Web sites

American Civil Liberties Union

http://www.aclu.org

The ACLU, the oldest and best-known civil-liberties organization, challenges governmental actions that, in its opinion, violate the Bill of Rights. ACLU lawyers handled Ernesto Miranda's appeal.

Heritage Foundation

http://www.heritage.org

This is one of the oldest and most influential conservative research and advocacy organizations. It supports law enforcement in criminal justice cases and has been critical of the *Miranda* rule.

Innocence Project

http://www.innocenceproject.org

This nonprofit legal clinic was established by two law professors and represents prisoners who, through postconviction DNA testing, can be proven innocent.

National Association of Criminal Defense Lawyers

http://www.nacdl.org

This is the leading national organization of defense lawyers. It favors measures to curb abusive interrogations, including videotaping of confessions and, when necessary, civil suits.

United States Justice Department

http://justice.gov

Headed by the attorney general, this is the Executive Branch department that is responsible for enforcing laws at the federal level. The FBI is part of the Justice Department.

Washington Legal Foundation

http://www.wlf.org

The WLF is a conservative public-interest law firm. It argued in *Dickerson* that *Miranda* should be overruled at a time when the administration refused to enforce §18 U.S.C. 3501. It supports broad Executive Branch powers to fight terrorism.

Cases

Brown v. Mississippi, 297 U.S. 278 (1936).
This ruling reversed the defendants' murder convictions because the police had obtained their confessions to the crime through torture and in doing so had denied the defendants due process of law.

Chavez v. Martinez, 538 U.S. 760 (2003).
The Court narrowly read the federal civil-rights statute and held that a police officer's aggressive interrogation of a suspect did not violate his Fifth Amendment rights because his statement was never used against him in a criminal trial.

Dickerson v. United States, 530 U.S. 428 (2000).
This case reaffirmed *Miranda*. It held that the *Miranda* rule was based on the Constitution and also held that 18 U.S.C. §3501 was an attempt to reimpose the pre-*Miranda* voluntariness standard and therefore was not enforceable.

Escobedo v. Illinois, 378 U.S. 478 (1964).
The majority held that, once a person became the "focus" of a criminal investigation, he or she had the right to consult with a lawyer before deciding whether to answer questions asked by the police.

Gideon v. Wainwright, 372 U.S. 335 (1963).
This ruling held that the Sixth Amendment right to the assistance of counsel applied to the states. The *Gideon* decision obligated the states to appoint a lawyer, at public expense, for a defendant who is charged with a serious crime and lacks the funds to hire a lawyer.

Harris v. New York, 401 U.S. 222 (1971).
This was the first major post-*Miranda* decision of the Supreme Court. The majority held that a statement obtained in violation of the *Miranda* rule could be used to cast doubt on the testimony of a defendant who testified in his own defense at his trial.

Malloy v. Hogan, 378 U.S. 1 (1964).
This ruling held that the Fifth Amendment privilege against self-incrimination applied to the states. Before *Malloy*, the Court decided whether to admit a defendant's confession under the due process clause. In doing so, it applied a general "voluntariness" standard.

Miranda v. Arizona, 384 U.S. 436 (1966).
The majority held that interrogation of a suspect who is in police custody was inherently coercive. To counteract that coercion, it required the police to warn the suspect that he or she had the right to remain silent and to have a lawyer present while being questioned.

Powell v. Alabama, 287 U.S. 45 (1932).
This was the first Supreme Court decision to overturn the rape convictions of the "Scottsboro Boys." Held that the defendants had not been given meaningful legal representation at their trial and therefore had been denied due process of law.

Stephan v. State, 711 P.2d 1156 (Alaska Sup. Ct. 1985).

This was the first decision by a state's highest court that required the police to record the interrogation of suspects. Stephan held that recording was required as a matter of due process of law.

Legislation and Provisions of the U.S. Constitution

18 U.S.C. §3501.

This provision, added to the federal criminal code two years after *Miranda*, attempted to reinstate the pre-*Miranda* "voluntariness" standard that governed confessions. In *Dickerson v. United States*, the Supreme Court refused to give it effect.

42 U.S.C §1983.

Part of the Civil Rights Act of 1871, it gives a citizen the right to sue a person who, while acting "under color of law," deprived him or her of constitutional or statutory rights. "Under color of law" means carrying out, or claiming to carry out, one's official duties.

Fifth Amendment

This amendment provides that no person may be compelled to be a witness against himself in a criminal case. The Supreme Court laid down the *Miranda* rule in an effort to protect suspects' Fifth Amendment rights.

Sixth Amendment

This amendment provides that a person accused of a crime has the right to "the assistance of counsel in his defence." This guarantee, which applies to court proceedings, was extended to interrogations in police custody by the *Escobedo* and *Miranda* decisions.

Fourteenth Amendment

The due process clause in §1 of the amendment forbids a state to deprive a person of life, liberty, or property without due process of law.

Terms and Concepts

Bill of Rights	interrogation
certiorari	judicial review
coercion	*Miranda* rule
common law	retroactivity
confession	right to counsel
criminal procedure	self-incrimination
due process clause	*stare decisis*
evidence	suppression
exclusionary rule	"third degree"
federalism	voluntariness standard
habeas corpus	waiver

How the Supreme Court Applied the Bill of Rights to State Criminal Cases

During the 2006 Republican primary election in Alabama, Supreme Court Justice Tom Parker, who was running for chief justice of that court, said, "State supreme court judges should not follow obviously wrong decisions simply because they are 'precedents'" and added that they "may decline to follow bad U.S. Supreme Court precedents because those decisions bind only the parties to the particular case."[1] In 2005, Justice Parker's anger at the Court reached a boiling point after the justices ruled in *Roper v. Simmons* that a state could not execute a murderer who was younger than 18 when he committed the crime, even if he had turned 18 before or during the trial.

Justice Parker's views are outside the legal mainstream, and few experts agree with him. (He lost in the primary.) They do show, however, that many Americans strongly resent federal intrusion into how a state chooses to govern itself—especially when the Supreme Court is the intruder. Hostility toward federal intervention is one reason many Americans believe that *Miranda* was wrongly decided.

For most of this country's history, a decision such as *Roper*—or, for that matter, *Miranda*—would have been unimaginable. The Supreme Court traditionally took a hands-off approach toward state criminal cases. That trend reversed itself in the early twentieth century and gained momentum during the 1960s, when many in the legal community believed that it was time to do away with unfairness in states' criminal justice systems.

States' rights has been a strong force in American law since the colonies won independence from Great Britain. At the Constitutional Convention of 1787, the Framers were concerned that a powerful central government could become a danger to liberty. They therefore gave the federal government power in certain specified areas, such as waging war and regulating commerce between the states, and left the states with the remaining powers. The powers retained by the states included so-called "police power": the authority to make laws for the public's health, safety, and welfare. As a result, the states were primarily responsible for defining crimes and administering criminal justice.

Many of the Framers thought that the Constitution itself contained enough safeguards against tyranny. Some, including James Madison, however, argued that the document should specifically guarantee individuals certain rights, especially in criminal cases. When the first Congress met, Madison introduced a resolution that would add the Bill of Rights to the

Constitution. The resolution passed and, in 1791, gained approval from the required number of states.

Most provisions of the Bill of Rights deal with criminal law. Two of them—the Fifth Amendment's prohibition of a person being "compelled in any criminal case to be a witness against himself" and the Sixth Amendment's guarantee that a person accused of a crime have "the Assistance of Counsel for his defence"—are critical to the *Miranda* decision.

At the time the Bill of Rights was adopted, the legal community believed that it restricted only the federal government. In 1833, in *Barron v. City of Baltimore*, the Supreme Court agreed. Any protection against the actions of state and local government had to be provided by state constitutions. Although most such constitutions had some version of a bill of rights, their provisions varied. In some states, they were very restrictive of government power; in others, they provided little or no protection.

Had *Barron* still been good law at the time of Ernesto Miranda's conviction, his appeal never would have reached the Supreme Court. A number of developments in the law spelled the end of *Barron*, however. The first occurred in 1868, when the Fourteenth Amendment became part of the Constitution. That amendment expanded the power of the federal government by requiring states to honor certain personal and property rights of their citizens. Section 1 provides in part, "No State shall make or enforce any law which shall abridge the privileges or immunities of citizens of the United States; nor shall any State deprive any person of life, liberty, or property, without due process of law; nor deny to any person within its jurisdiction the equal protection of the laws."[2]

Despite the sweeping language of the due process clause, a conservative Supreme Court read those provisions narrowly, especially in criminal cases. It took two racially charged trials to prod the justices into applying the due process clause to overturn convictions in state courts. In *Powell v. Alabama*, the Court reversed the rape convictions of four young African-American men because they had not been given effective legal representation at their trial. Four years later, in *Brown v. Mississippi*, the Court reversed the murder convictions of three African-American sharecroppers because their confessions had been obtained by torture.

Although the Court had signaled its willingness to reverse unjust convictions, it otherwise held fast to its position that specific provisions of the Bill of Rights applied in federal prosecutions only. The justices left it up to state courts and lawmakers to decide how to punish police officers who illegally obtained evidence, who was entitled to a jury trial and to have a court-appointed lawyer, and what kind of sentence to impose on those convicted. In doing so, they followed *Hurtado v. California* (1884), in which the Court rejected the argument that the Bill of Rights was "incorporated" into the due process clause. The only dissenter in *Hurtado*, John Harlan, believed otherwise. He argued that the similarity of language in the due process clause in the Fifth Amendment and that in the Fourteenth Amendment "evinces a purpose to impose upon the States the same restrictions, in respect of proceedings involving life, liberty, and property, which had been imposed upon the general government."[3] Harlan's grandson, also named John Harlan, would be a dissenter in *Miranda*.

Over time, the first Justice Harlan's view largely became the law of the land. The process of applying the Bill of Rights to the states took decades, however. In 1925, the Court took the first step, stating that "for present purposes we may and do assume that freedom of speech and of the press—which are protected by the First Amendment from abridgment by Congress—are among the fundamental personal rights and 'liberties' protected by the due process clause of the Fourteenth Amendment from impairment by the States."[4] A dozen years later, the Court adopted the doctrine of "selective incorporation." It reasoned that the due process clause includes "the specific pledges of particular amendments have been found to be implicit in the concept of ordered liberty, and thus, through the Fourteenth Amendment, become valid as against the states."[5]

Under that standard, key provisions of the Bill of Rights—including the privilege against self-incrimination and the right to counsel, as well as the exclusionary rule, which penalized the authorities with the loss of unlawfully obtained evidence—were not considered incorporated into the due process clause. The Court reversed itself during the "due process revolution" of the 1960s, when a majority of the Court, led by Chief Justice Earl Warren, swept aside earlier holdings. *Mapp v. Ohio* (1961), which imposed the exclusionary rule on the states in search-and-seizure cases, overturned a 12-year-old decision that went the other way. *Gideon v. Wainwright* (1963), which required states to appoint a lawyer for a person charged with a serious crime, overruled a decision handed down 19 years earlier. *Malloy v. Hogan* (1964), which held that the Fifth Amendment applied to the states, reversed a contrary decision from 17 years earlier. This was unusual behavior for a Court that has historically been reluctant to depart from earlier rulings. For that reason, those decisions proved highly controversial.

Malloy and *Gideon* are significant to *Miranda* because the privilege against self-incrimination and the right to counsel were about to come together. *Escobedo v. Illinois* held that, when a person became the "focus" of a criminal investigation and was being questioned by the police, he or she had the right to consult with a lawyer. In the eyes of many, *Miranda* was the next logical step after *Escobedo*. Some thought—or feared—that the Court intended to expand on *Miranda* and require that a lawyer be present in the stationhouse when a suspect was questioned or even ban in-custody questioning altogether. What supporters and opponents did not realize at the time was that *Miranda* was the last major criminal case the Warren Court would decide.

1. Jay Reeves, "Alabama Candidates Revive Judicial Debate," Associated Press, May 31, 2006.
2. U.S. Const. amend. XIV., §1.
3. 110 U.S. 516, 541 (Harlan, J., dissenting).
4. *Gitlow v. New York*, 268 U.S. 652, 666 (1925).
5. *Palko v. Connecticut*, 302 U.S. 319, 324-25 (1937).

Beginning Legal Research

The goal of POINT/COUNTERPOINT is not only to provide the reader with an introduction to a controversial issue affecting society, but also to encourage the reader to explore the issue more fully. This appendix, then, is meant to serve as a guide to the reader in researching the current state of the law as well as exploring some of the public-policy arguments as to why existing laws should be changed or new laws are needed.

Like many types of research, legal research has become much faster and more accessible with the invention of the Internet. This appendix discusses some of the best starting points, but of course "surfing the Net" will uncover endless additional sources of information—some more reliable than others. Some important sources of law are not yet available on the Internet, but these can generally be found at the larger public and university libraries. Librarians usually are happy to point patrons in the right direction.

The most important source of law in the United States is the Constitution. Originally enacted in 1787, the Constitution outlines the structure of our federal government and sets limits on the types of laws that the federal government and state governments can pass. Through the centuries, a number of amendments have been added to or changed in the Constitution, most notably the first ten amendments, known collectively as the Bill of Rights, which guarantee important civil liberties. Each state also has its own constitution, many of which are similar to the U.S. Constitution. It is important to be familiar with the U.S. Constitution because so many of our laws are affected by its requirements. State constitutions often provide protections of individual rights that are even stronger than those set forth in the U.S. Constitution.

Within the guidelines of the U.S. Constitution, Congress—both the House of Representatives and the Senate—passes bills that are either vetoed or signed into law by the President. After the passage of the law, it becomes part of the United States Code, which is the official compilation of federal laws. The state legislatures use a similar process, in which bills become law when signed by the state's governor. Each state has its own official set of laws, some of which are published by the state and some of which are published by commercial publishers. The U.S. Code and the state codes are an important source of legal research; generally, legislators make efforts to make the language of the law as clear as possible.

However, reading the text of a federal or state law generally provides only part of the picture. In the American system of government, after the legislature passes laws and the executive (U.S. President or state governor) signs them, it is up to the judicial branch of the government, the court system, to interpret the laws and decide whether they violate any provision of the Constitution. At the state level, each state's supreme court has the ultimate authority in determining what a law means and whether or not it violates the state constitution. However, the federal courts—headed by the U.S. Supreme Court—can review state laws and court decisions to determine whether they violate federal laws or the U.S. Constitution. For example, a state court may find that a particular criminal law is valid under the state's constitution, but a federal court may then review the state court's decision and determine that the law is invalid under the U.S. Constitution.

It is important, then, to read court decisions when doing legal research. The Constitution uses language that is intentionally very general—for example, prohibiting "unreasonable searches and seizures" by the police—and court cases often provide more guidance. For example, the U.S. Supreme Court's 2001 decision in *Kyllo* v. *United States* held that scanning the outside of a person's house using a heat sensor to determine whether the person is growing marijuana is unreasonable—*if* it is done without a search warrant secured from a judge. Supreme Court decisions provide the most definitive explanation of the law of the land, and it is therefore important to include these in research. Often, when the Supreme Court has not decided a case on a particular issue, a decision by a federal appeals court or a state supreme court can provide guidance; but just as laws and constitutions can vary from state to state, so can federal courts be split on a particular interpretation of federal law or the U.S. Constitution. For example, federal appeals courts in Louisiana and California may reach opposite conclusions in similar cases.

Lawyers and courts refer to statutes and court decisions through a formal system of citations. Use of these citations reveals which court made the decision (or which legislature passed the statute) and when and enables the reader to locate the statute or court case quickly in a law library. For example, the legendary Supreme Court case *Brown* v. *Board of Education* has the legal citation 347 U.S. 483 (1954). At a law library, this 1954 decision can be found on page 483 of volume 347 of the U.S. Reports, the official collection of the Supreme Court's decisions. Citations can also be helpful in locating court cases on the Internet.

Understanding the current state of the law leads only to a partial understanding of the issues covered by the POINT/COUNTERPOINT series. For a fuller understanding of the issues, it is necessary to look at public-policy arguments that the current state of the law is not adequately addressing the issue.

Many groups lobby for new legislation or changes to existing legislation; the National Rifle Association (NRA), for example, lobbies Congress and the state legislatures constantly to make existing gun control laws less restrictive and not to pass additional laws. The NRA and other groups dedicated to various causes might also intervene in pending court cases: a group such as Planned Parenthood might file a brief *amicus curiae* (as "a friend of the court")—called an "amicus brief"—in a lawsuit that could affect abortion rights. Interest groups also use the media to influence public opinion, issuing press releases and frequently appearing in interviews on news programs and talk shows. The books in POINT/COUNTERPOINT list some of the interest groups that are active in the issue at hand, but in each case there are countless other groups working at the local, state, and national levels. It is important to read everything with a critical eye, for sometimes interest groups present information in a way that can be read only to their advantage. The informed reader must always look for bias.

Finding sources of legal information on the Internet is relatively simple thanks to "portal" sites such as FindLaw (*www.findlaw.com*), which provides access to a variety of constitutions, statutes, court opinions, law review articles, news articles, and other resources—including all Supreme Court decisions issued since 1893. Other useful sources of information include the U.S. Government Printing Office (*www.gpo.gov*), which contains a complete copy of the U.S. Code, and the Library of Congress's THOMAS system (*thomas.loc.gov*), which offers access to bills pending before Congress as well as recently passed laws. Of course, the Internet changes every second of every day, so it is best to do some independent searching. Most cases, studies, and opinions that are cited or referred to in public debate can be found online—and *everything* can be found in one library or another.

The Internet can provide a basic understanding of most important legal issues, but not all sources can be found there. To find some documents it is necessary to visit the law library of a university or a public law library; some cities have public law libraries, and many library systems keep legal documents at the main branch. On the following page are some common citation forms.

COMMON CITATION FORMS

Source of Law	Sample Citation	Notes
U.S. Supreme Court	*Employment Division v. Smith*, 485 U.S. 660 (1988)	The U.S. Reports is the official record of Supreme Court decisions. There is also an unofficial Supreme Court ("S. Ct.") reporter.
U.S. Court of Appeals	*United States v. Lambert*, 695 F.2d 536 (11th Cir.1983)	Appellate cases appear in the Federal Reporter, designated by "F." The 11th Circuit has jurisdiction in Alabama, Florida, and Georgia.
U.S. District Court	*Carillon Importers, Ltd. v. Frank Pesce Group, Inc.*, 913 F.Supp. 1559 (S.D.Fla.1996)	Federal trial-level decisions are reported in the Federal Supplement ("F. Supp."). Some states have multiple federal districts; this case originated in the Southern District of Florida.
U.S. Code	Thomas Jefferson Commemoration Commission Act, 36 U.S.C., §149 (2002)	Sometimes the popular names of legislation—names with which the public may be familiar—are included with the U.S. Code citation.
State Supreme Court	*Sterling v. Cupp*, 290 Ore. 611, 614, 625 P.2d 123, 126 (1981)	The Oregon Supreme Court decision is reported in both the state's reporter and the Pacific regional reporter.
State Statute	Pennsylvania Abortion Control Act of 1982, 18 Pa. Cons. Stat. 3203-3220 (1990)	States use many different citation formats for their statutes.

PICTURE CREDITS

PAUL RUSCHMANN, J.D., is a legal analyst and writer based in Canton, Michigan. He received his undergraduate degree from the University of Notre Dame and his law degree from the University of Michigan. He is a member of the State Bar of Michigan. His areas of specialization include legislation, public safety, traffic and transportation, and trade regulation. He is also the author of six other titles in the POINT/COUNTERPOINT series: *Legalizing Marijuana, Mandatory Military Service, The War on Terror, Media Bias, Tort Reform*, and *The FCC and Regulating Indecency*. He can be found online at www.PaulRuschmann.com.

ALAN MARZILLI, M.A., J.D., lives in Washington, D.C., and is a program associate with Advocates for Human Potential, Inc., a research and consulting firm based in Sudbury, Mass., and Albany, N.Y. He primarily works on developing training and educational materials for agencies of the Federal government on topics such as housing, mental health policy, employment, and transportation. He has spoken on mental health issues in thirty states, the District of Columbia, and Puerto Rico; his work has included training mental health administrators, nonprofit management and staff, and people with mental illnesses and their families on a wide variety of topics, including effective advocacy, community-based mental health services, and housing. He has written several handbooks and training curricula that are used nationally—as far away as the territory of Guam. He managed statewide and national mental health advocacy programs and worked for several public interest lobbying organizations while studying law at Georgetown University. He has written more than a dozen books, including numerous titles in the *Point/Counterpoint* series.